SNAPSHOT

Pre-Intermediate

Students'
Book

Brian Abbs

Ingrid Freebairn

Chris Barker

Longman

Contents

Vocabulary	Skills	Helpline	Soundbite
Noun formation with -er, -r and -or Jobs and occupations	**Speaking: see 'Communication'** Read an interview with an Italian student working in Britain as a lifeguard Listen to an interview with an instructor Write an interview with a person about their job	Speaking Keep a conversation going	Weak form / ə / in two-syllable words: sing**er**, sail**or**
Past time adverbials: *yesterday (afternoon),* *last (week), (a month) ago,* *this (morning)* Means of transport	Read a letter from Nicola to a friend from home Write a letter about a journey Read an article about some girl mountaineers Listen to someone talking about a climbing incident	Writing Informal letters	Elision: the sound / dʒ / as in /ˈdɪdʒʊ/ Did you like it?
Revision			
The natural environment	Read about Cornwall Read about people's holiday plans Listen to a girl talking about her holiday plans Write about holiday plans	Writing Collect and organise ideas	Falling intonation on *Wh-* questions: What are you doing on Saturday?
Adjectives with negative prefixes: *un-, in-, im-*	Read about surfing Listen to a surfer Write quiz answers expressing your opinion	Writing Express opinions	Word stress in adjectives: popular, unpopular
Revision			

Verbs of movement: *dive, jump, leap,* etc.	Read about a dramatic rescue in a marina Listen to someone describing a frightening incident Write paragraphs about an incident Write directions		The sound / ŋ /: work**ing** wait**ing** hav**ing**
Clothes and parts of clothes Humour	Listen to a radio interview with some tourists in London Write a postcard about a stay in a capital city Read about comedy and an interview with the actor who plays Mr Bean	Reading Use visual clues to help you read	Falling intonation with question tags: You're Nicola, aren't you?
Revision			
Verbs connected with food and cooking	Listen to a dialogue about a household incident Read about a hiccups attack	Listening Use visual context to help you listen	Elision between two consonants: baked potatoes fried bread
Nouns and adjectives of emotion	Read about bullying Listen to a boy talking about a bullying incident Write a letter	Vocabulary Increase your word power	Weak form / bɪn /: Have you **been** waiting long?
Revision			

	Unit	Communication	Grammar
11	**Unless I get to bed, ...**	Talk about future possibility Show surprise	Verbs *will/won't, may* or *might* for predictions First conditional: *if/unless* clause + *'ll (will)/won't* Negative questions
12	**They were delivered today.**	Describe processes Complain, request and apologise	The passive: present and past simple
	Fast rewind: Units 11 and 12	Revision	Revision
13	**If I had the money, ...**	Talk about imaginary situations in the future Ask for and give advice	Pronouns: *some-, any-, no-, every-* + *thing, one, whe* Second conditional: *if* clause + *'d (would)/wouldn'*
14	**Someone had dropped it.**	Talk about events before other events in the past Express pleasure and thanks	Past perfect simple *too many, too much, not enough* Reported requests and commands (verb + object + infinitive)
	Fast rewind: Units 13 and 14	Revision	Revision
15	**Wide angle: A circus with a difference** **Project 3:** Snapshot of food and drink **Take a break 3: Song** – *When I'm sixty-four*		Consolidation of language and skills
16	**They used to hide here.**	Talk about past habits Buy tickets	Verb *used to* *so* and *such a/an* + adjective + noun for exclamations *so* and *such* with a clause of result
17	**He said he'd been away.**	Report what people said Using the telephone	Reported statements
	Fast rewind: Units 16 and 17	Revision	Revision
18	**'The Birds'**	Report what people asked Ask permission with *Do you mind/ Is it all right if I ... ?*	Reported questions
19	**He's too good to fall.**	Say the right thing	*too* + adjective/adverb + *to* *(not)* + adjective/adverb + *enough to* Verb + infinitive/gerund
	Fast rewind: Units 18 and 19	Revision	Revision
20	**Wide angle: The boy who was taught to talk by dolphins** **Project 4:** Snapshot of inventions **Take a break 4: Song** – *I will survive*		Consolidation of language and skills

Vocabulary	Skills	Helpline	Soundbite

Verb *get*
Parts of the body
	Speaking: see 'Communication'
	
	Write a paragraph about a future event
	Read an article about truths and myths
	  about your body
	Listen to a gymnast talking about training
		Vocabulary
		Record meanings in
		  sentences
			The sound / I / in
			initial, medial and
			final position:
			Let's Nicola I'll

Adjectives to describe
  behaviour
	Read about battery hens and
	  factory farming
	Listen to a farmer talking about modern
	  farming methods
	Write a letter of protest about animal cruelty
		Writing
		Formal letters
			Syllable deletion:
			  interested
			  difference

Revision			
Personality adjectives: *sensitive, aggressive*, etc.	Read about people's dreams and ambitions Write about your dreams and ambitions Listen to a radio programme Read and complete a questionnaire	Writing Check written work	Intonation of conditionals: If I were you, I wouldn't do anything
Types of music	Read about a visit to a weekend pop festival Listen to people describing a pop festival Write a paragraph describing an incident	Reading Skimreading	Sentence stress: He <u>told</u> us to <u>stop</u>.
Revision			

Vocabulary	Skills	Helpline	Soundbite

Word building from
  different parts of speech
	Read about smuggling in Cornwall
	Write about smuggling in Cornwall
	Write about childhood memories
	Listen to conversation about the way
	  a boy has changed
			Emphatic stress
			  with *so* and *such*

Noun formation with endings:
  -ment, -ion, -er, -ance
	Read about the Italian inventor, Marconi
	Listen to a guided tour
	Write about an inventor
		Vocabulary
		Use word endings to
		  identify parts of speech
			Rising intonation in
			telephone conversations:
			Hello Who's speaking?

Revision			

Phrases of approximate time
  and quantity: *a few*
  (*minutes ago*), *about, a couple
  of, several, lots of* (*people*), etc.
	Read an extract from a short story, *The Birds*
	Listen to how the story ends
	Write the next paragraph of the story
	Listen to an interview with someone who
	  wants to be a vet
		Speaking
		Express mood
		  through intonation
			Rising intonation
			to ask polite questions:
			Do you mind if I sit here?

Neutral and strong adjectives	Read an interview with a film star Listen to people saying 'Goodbye'	Revision Keep up your English	Sentence stress: He's <u>too</u> good to <u>fall</u>. He's <u>not good</u> enough to <u>win</u>.
Revision			

Lynn Tremayne · Nicola Jones · Jake Preston · Louise Morgan

Tom Penhale   Jamie Penhale   Steve Penhale   June Penhale

1 I'm here to work.

Bus Stop

Western National

Customer Helplines
● Bodmin   (01208) 79898
● Camborne (01209) 719988

Learning goals

Communication
Give personal information
Show interest or surprise

Grammar
Present simple and continuous
Echo questions
Infinitive of purpose

Vocabulary
Noun formation with -er, -r and -or
Jobs and occupations

1 🔊 Listen and read

Jake: Excuse me. Which bus do I take to get to Fistral Beach?
Nicola: You need a number 53.
Jake: Are you waiting for the 53 too?
Nicola: Yes, I am. Are you a surfer?
Jake: Yes. I'm here for the surfing championships.
Nicola: Where do you come from?
Jake: Cape Town. I'm in the South African surfing team.
Nicola: Are you? Brilliant!
Jake: What about you? Do you live here?
Nicola: No. I live in London.
Jake: Do you? Are you in Newquay on holiday?
Nicola: No. I usually come here on holiday with my parents, but this time I'm here to work.
Jake: Really? Hard luck!
Nicola: I don't mind. It's a part-time holiday job at a hotel. My aunt's the manager there. Oh, here comes our bus.

2 Comprehension

Answer T (true) or F (false).

1 Jake knows Nicola.
2 Jake is on a school trip.
3 Jake is South African.
4 Nicola is in Newquay on holiday.
5 This is her first time in Newquay.
6 Nicola's aunt works in a hotel.
7 Nicola and Jake are going to travel on the same bus.

3 🔊 Useful phrases

Listen and repeat.

- Excuse me. • Brilliant! • Really?
- Hard luck! • I don't mind.
- Here comes [our bus].

4 Vocabulary

Noun formation with *-er, -r* **and** *-or*

Many nouns can be formed from verbs by adding *-er, -r* or *-or* to the main verb. These nouns usually refer to people or jobs.

- surf – surfer   • manage – manager
- act – actor   • run – runner

Use a dictionary to find the nouns which come from these verbs. Then say what each person does.

1 build   2 drum   3 sail   4 drive
5 sing   6 conduct   7 dive   8 report

1 builder: A builder builds houses.
2 drummer: A drummer plays the drums.

5 🔊 Soundbite

Weak form / ə / in two-syllable words

sing**er**   sail**or**   (Look at page 122.)

6 Memory bank

Jobs and occupations

1 How many jobs can you list in two minutes?
2 Talk about the jobs of three people you know. Say where they work.
3 Which job would you like? Why?

Ryan Carter

Michelle Grant

Grammar snapshot

Present simple and continuous

a> Which tenses are used in the sentences below?
1 I **come** from South Africa.
2 I'm **waiting** for a bus.
3 We usually **come** here every summer.
4 They're **working** in a hotel for the summer.

b> Go back and look.
Find examples of the present simple and continuous in the dialogue in Exercise 1.

c> Make rules.
1 We use the ... for permanent situations and routines.
2 We use the ... for activities that are happening at or around the time of speaking.

d> What's the difference in meaning?
1 She **works** in a hotel.
2 She**'s working** in a hotel.

Snapshot of part-time jobs

Michelle Grant goes to a High School in San Francisco, California, USA.

'At the moment I'm doing a part-time job to earn some extra money. I'm working as a waitress in a pizza restaurant. I work on Friday and Saturday evenings and get $60 at the end of it. I take orders and serve food. It's really hard work but at least I get free pizzas! I often sing when I'm working. In my spare time I sing in a choir.'

7> Practice

Complete the sentences with the present simple or the present continuous.

1 'What's that terrible noise?' 'My brother is having a singing lesson today!'

1 'What's that terrible noise?' 'My brother (have) ... a singing lesson today!'
2 'How many languages (speak) ... your brother ... ?' 'Two. And he (learn) ... Russian at the moment.'
3 'Where (have lunch) ... she usually ... ?' 'She (always/go home) ... .'
4 'Where's Sally?' 'She (play) ... tennis in the park. She (play) ... every Friday.'
5 '(teach) ... they ... Russian in your school?' 'No, they ... .'
6 'What's the lovely smell?' 'My Dad (cook) ... hamburgers on the barbecue.'

8> Interaction

Student B: Turn to page 121.
Student A: Ask Student B questions about Ryan and complete the chart. Then read about Michelle and answer Student B's questions.

A: *Where does Ryan come from?*
B: *He comes from ... .*
A: *What part-time job is he doing at the moment?*
B: *...*
A: *What sort of things does he do in his job?*
   When does he work?
   How much does he earn?
   What does he like about the job?
   What does he do in his free time?

Ryan
Home town/city:
Part-time job:
Duties:
Work days:
Pay:
Best part of job:
Other interests:

9〉 Speaking helpline

Keep a conversation going

When you are having a conversation, you can show surprise or interest in the other person by using 'echo' questions, like *Is it?*, *Are you?*, *Do you?*, *Have you?* as well as phrases like *Really?*, *That's interesting.* and *Oh, yes?*

10〉 Communication

Showing interest or surprise

▶ Do you live near here?
▶ Yes, I live in the next street.
▶ Do you? I live miles away.

▶ How many brothers and sisters have you got?
▶ I've got four brothers.
▶ Have you? I'm an only child.

In pairs, have similar conversations. Then continue with the questions below and any other questions you want to ask.

● How do you get to school?
● Which subjects do you like best at school?
● What do you like doing in your free time?
● Who's your favourite band?
● Are you doing a part-time job at the moment? (What? Where? When? How much/earn?)

Grammar flash

Infinitive of purpose
I'm here **to work**.
He's here **to earn** some money.

11〉 Practice

Look at the people in the pictures below and make sentences using an infinitive of purpose.

1 They're staying in a youth hostel to save money.

We're saving money. That's why we're staying in a youth hostel.

1

I'm learning English. I go to classes twice a week.

2

I'm competing in a surfing contest. That's why I'm in Cornwall.

3

We're visiting relatives. That's why we're in the UK.

4

I'm earning some extra money. That's why I've got a job as a waitress.

5

11

Summer Jobs

Jan Baxter meets Gianni Zuccarello, 20, a young Italian who is working in Newquay for the summer.

○ **Where do you come from?**

I come from Rimini. It's a seaside resort on the east coast of Italy.

○ **What are you doing in Newquay?**

I'm working as a lifeguard on the main beach for the summer season.

○ **Why are you here?**

I'm here to improve my English, to earn some money and to do something useful during my holidays. This is just a summer job. It's not a career.

○ **Do you go to college back home in Italy?**

Yes, I do. I'm a student at a technical college in Rome. I'm studying electronics.

○ **What are your qualifications for this job?**

I'm a good swimmer and I'm fit. I've also got a life-saving certificate.

○ **What are your working hours?**

There are four of us and we work shifts. I usually start work at 9 a.m. and finish at 2 p.m. but I sometimes work from 2 p.m. to 8 p.m. I earn £200 a week. That's good money for a summer job.

○ **What do you like about being a lifeguard?**

You meet people from all over the world – that's interesting – and every day you help people. I like being near the sea and I like all water sports, especially windsurfing. And, of course, you get a tan and meet lots of girls!

○ **Is there anything you don't like about the job?**

I don't like it when the weather's bad. Then my job is really boring.

Before you read

Do students do summer jobs in your country?
What kind of jobs do they have?

12〉 Read

Read the interview and complete the information.

NEWQUAY BEACH LIFEGUARDS	
NAME:	*Gianni Zuccarello*
NATIONALITY:	
HOME TOWN/CITY:	
LANGUAGES:	
JOB:	
SHIFTS:	
PAY:	

13〉 ⊙⊙ Listen

Listen to an interview with Eva and answer the questions.

1 Where does Eva come from?
2 What is her job in Britain?
3 What does she do part-time?
4 How often does she do this?
5 What are her qualifications?
6 How does she help beginners?
7 What makes the job difficult?
8 How much does she earn?
9 What does she save her money for?

14〉 Write

a〉 Use questions from the interview with Gianni to write a similar interview with someone who has a part-time job.

b〉 Write about yourself.

Mention your age, family, school, friends and hobbies. Write about the sports you do and any part-time job you are doing.

On the bus

Read the story and put the sentences at the bottom of the page in the correct places. Then listen and see if you were right.

1

My name's Jake, by the way. ____?

Nicola.

2

____?

Yes, I do. It gets very crowded in the summer but there are some great clubs here.

3

____?

They're unloading crabs. The fishing boats usually come in at about this time.

4

____. Good luck in the championships!

Thanks. Here, let me help you with that case.

5

Come and watch our surfing team one day.

Is that an invitation?

____.

6

Hello, Auntie Lynn. I'm here at last!

Nicola! ____!

7

How's business?

____. The hotel's full.

____? That's good.

Yes, we're doing really well.

- Fine. - Yes, it is. - How lovely to see you! - Is it? - What's your name?
- Do you like Newquay? - What are they doing in the harbour? - Here's my stop.

2 Over three hours late.

Learning goals

Communication
Talk about past journeys

Grammar
Past simple of regular and irregular verbs
Conjunctions *so* and *because*
Linkers: *first (of all), then, before (breakfast),*
after (that), later, the next day, in the end

Vocabulary
Past time adverbials:
yesterday (afternoon), last (week),
(a month) ago, this (morning)
Means of transport

Cliff Hotel
Headland Road,
Newquay,
Cornwall
TR7 1HN

Telephone (01637) 873690

Friday 17th July

Dear Suzy,
Thanks for your letter. It was great to hear from you.
Well I'm here in Newquay at last! I arrived this morning at 11.30. Believe it or not, the journey took twelve hours altogether from London. It wasn't much fun. In fact it was a nightmare!
First of all the other girl in the sleeping compartment complained because she didn't have the bottom bunk and then, when she climbed up to go to bed, she almost stepped on my face! Later, when I went to the toilet in the night, I tripped over my shoes (you know how clumsy I am!) and the noise woke her up.
After that there was a signal failure near Plymouth and the train stopped for ages. Luckily there was a phone on the train so I phoned my aunt and told her about the delay. In the end I was over three hours late when I got to Newquay. But guess what? I met a really nice South African guy at the bus stop near the station. He's a surfer. He's called Jake and he's cool.
I'm starting my holiday job tomorrow so I'm going to relax and take things easy this afternoon.

Write soon!

Love,
Nicola

14

1 ⟨••⟩ Read

Read Nicola's letter and answer the questions.

1 What time did the train leave London?
2 Why was the other girl in the compartment unhappy?
3 How did she annoy Nicola?
4 In what way was Nicola clumsy?
5 Why did Nicola use the phone on the train?
6 What happened at the bus stop?

2 ⟨••⟩ Listen and read

Lynn: So, Nicola, how was your journey?
Nicola: It was pretty bad but it could have been worse.
Tom: Here's your coffee, Mrs Tremayne.
Lynn: Thanks, Tom. Nicola, this is Tom. He's at Newquay High School. He's got a summer job at the hotel, too. He started a week ago.
Tom: Hi! What time did you arrive?
Nicola: About two hours ago.
Lynn: Oh, look, there's Louise! She's staying here with her parents. I think she's a bit lonely.
Tom: I must serve coffee to the other guests. See you later, Nicola.
Nicola: OK. Bye, Tom! Nice to meet you.
Lynn: Louise! Come and meet my niece, Nicola.

3 ⟩ Comprehension

Put the sentences into the correct order to summarise the story.

1b) Tom starts work at the Cliff Hotel in Newquay.

a) Nicola meets Tom and Louise.
b) Tom starts work at the Cliff Hotel in Newquay.
c) Nicola leaves London.
d) Nicola meets Jake at the bus stop near the station.
e) Nicola arrives at the hotel and meets her aunt.
f) Nicola has an unpleasant train journey to Cornwall.

4 ⟨••⟩ Useful phrases

Listen and repeat.

- It could have been worse.
- Here's [your coffee].
- Oh, look, there's [Louise]!
- See you later.
- Bye! Nice to meet you.
- Come and meet [my niece, Nicola].

Grammar snapshot

Past simple of regular and irregular verbs
I **arrived** at nine o'clock.
I **left** at ten o'clock.

a> Compare the sentences above.
1 What are the infinitive forms of the two verbs?
2 In what way are the two past forms different?

b> Go back and look.
Find all the past tense verbs in the letter in
Exercise 1 and the dialogue in Exercise 2.

c> Make rules.
1 To make the regular positive past tense ending,
   we add ... or ... .
2 To make negatives, questions and short answers,
   we use the auxiliary verb ... .

5> Vocabulary   Past time adverbials

Complete the past time adverbial phrases in
the chart below using the correct time word.

- ago • on • in • at • last • this • yesterday

yesterday morning

...	morning	...	morning	...	night
	afternoon		afternoon		week
	evening		evening		weekend
			week		month
			month		year
					February
...	Friday, July 10th	...	August		
	Saturday night		1998		
			June 1999		
	five minutes	...	...	three o'clock	
	two hours			midday	
	two days			midnight	
	a week				
	three months				

6> Practice

Complete the sentences with the past tense of the
verb in brackets and the correct time adverbial.

1 Nicola arrived in Newquay a few hours ago.

1 Nicola (arrive) ... in Newquay a few hours ... .
2 Louise's parents first (come) ... to the Cliff Hotel
   ... 1995.
3 We (not/watch) ... TV ... night.
4 Louise (go) ... to see the new Tom Cruise film ...
   evening.
5 Tom's school term (finish) ... ... midday ... 4th July.
6 My grandfather (die) ... ... August 1997.

7> ⦂⦂ Soundbite

Elision: the sound / dʒ / as in / ˈdɪdʒʊ /
Di**d y**ou like it? (Look at page 122.)

8> Over to you

Ask ten questions about your partner's past.
Then tell the class at least one interesting fact
about your partner.

Grammar flash

Conjunctions *so* **and** *because*

It was very noisy **so** I didn't sleep very well.
I didn't sleep very well **because** it was very noisy.

So describes a consequence; *because* describes a reason.

9 Practice

Join the sentences in two ways, with *so* **and** *because.*

1 It started to rain so we went back home.
We went back home because it started to rain.

1 It started to rain. We went back home.
2 I went to bed late last night. I slept late this morning.
3 He couldn't find his pen. He wrote his homework in pencil.
4 There was nothing good on TV. They decided to rent a video.
5 The fans started to fight. The police came on to the pitch.

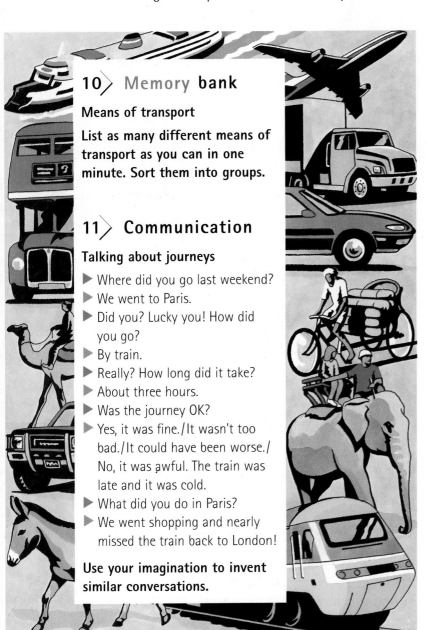

10 Memory bank

Means of transport

List as many different means of transport as you can in one minute. Sort them into groups.

11 Communication

Talking about journeys

▶ Where did you go last weekend?
▶ We went to Paris.
▶ Did you? Lucky you! How did you go?
▶ By train.
▶ Really? How long did it take?
▶ About three hours.
▶ Was the journey OK?
▶ Yes, it was fine./It wasn't too bad./It could have been worse./No, it was awful. The train was late and it was cold.
▶ What did you do in Paris?
▶ We went shopping and nearly missed the train back to London!

Use your imagination to invent similar conversations.

12 Writing helpline

Informal letters

Say if the following are used in formal (F) or informal (I) letters.

---

1 Date
a) July 13th 199...
b) Tues, July 7th
c) Friday afternoon

2 Greeting
a) Dear Jake,
b) Hi, Nicola!
c) Dear Sir,

3 Opening
a) Thanks for your card.
b) Thank you for your letter of July 5th.
c) It was great to hear from you.

4 Closing
a) Hope to hear from you soon.
b) I look forward to hearing from you.
c) Write soon!

5 Ending
a) Yours faithfully, L. Tremayne
b) Best wishes, Tom
c) Love, Marta

---

13 Write

Write an informal letter to a penfriend about a real or imaginary journey. You can use Nicola's letter in Exercise 1 as a model to help you. Include past time adverbials, and join the events with conjunctions and some of these linkers.

• first of all
• then
• after/before (breakfast)
• after/before (that)
• later
• the next day/morning
• in the end

Climbing is our life

Last summer Annabelle Jones and Claire Hippert, two 17-year-old English schoolgirls, decided to climb the Matterhorn, the famous snow-covered mountain in Switzerland. The Matterhorn is popular with mountain climbers because it is so difficult to climb.

The girls first got the idea for a climbing expedition a few years ago, when a well-known disabled climber, Norman Croucher, gave a talk at their school. Norman lost both his legs in a train accident when he was nineteen, but he has climbed some of the world's highest mountains on his artificial legs. 'He inspired us,' said Claire.

Then the girls met a well-known mountaineer called Turbo Thomas and he became their trainer. For the next two years he took them climbing in the Swiss Alps during the summer holidays and they trained very hard. 'It wasn't easy,' said Annabelle. 'The weather was often a problem.

Sometimes it was freezing cold and we didn't want to get out of bed, but Turbo dragged us to the foot of the mountain and made us climb.'

The girls kept going and finally they were ready to try the Matterhorn. They made a date for the last week in August and travelled to Zermatt. They started to climb but unfortunately the weather beat them. 'It rained every day so it was impossible to climb very far,' said Claire.

Are they disappointed? 'Definitely not,' said Annabelle. 'I know we didn't get to the top, but we'll be back next summer to try again! Climbing is our life.'

> **Left:** Norman Croucher
> **Centre:** Annabelle at the foot of the Matterhorn
> **Below:** Claire and Annabelle

14 Read

a Read the article and complete the chart.

Names of climbers:	1	2
Ages:		
Nationality:		
Occupation:		
Trainer:		
Mountain attempted:		
Country:		

b Answer the questions.

1 Why did the girls start mountain climbing?
2 Where and how did they train?
3 Why was the training difficult?
4 Did they climb the Matterhorn?
5 Why are they going to return to Zermatt next summer?

15 Listen

Chris and his friends Ben and Nick planned to do a walk to a mountain called Scafell Pike. Listen and answer the questions.

1 What was the weather like at the beginning?
2 What did they take with them?
3 How did the weather change?
4 What did Ben and Chris feel was wrong?
5 How did they find the way back?
6 What lesson did they learn?

16 Discussion

When do accidents happen on mountains? Why?
What do people often fail to do?

Fast rewind UNITS 1 and 2

Grammar

1 Complete the sentences with the present simple or present continuous form of the verb in brackets.

What ... your brother ... today? (do)
What is your brother doing today?

1 My mother ... coffee. (not drink)
2 Where ... he ... in South Africa? (come from)
3 My parents ... in Scotland at the moment. (climb)
4 ... they ... football every Saturday? (play)
5 Anna usually ... her homework in bed. (do)
6 ... they ... a good holiday? (have)

2 Complete the text with the correct verbs in the past tense.

• think • put out • can • be • jump • run • wake
• lose • survive • realise • phone • arrive • scream

When Sam Collins [1] *woke* up early one morning last year, she [2] ... it was just another day. 'But then I [3] ... smell smoke. I [4] ... the awful truth. Our house [5] ... on fire! I [6] ... out of bed and [7] ... "Fire!" Mum quickly [8] ... the fire brigade and we all [9] ... outside. The fire engine [10] ... in a few minutes and [11] ... the fire. I [12] ... all my clothes in the fire but at least we all [13] ... .'

3 Rewrite the sentences using an infinitive of purpose.

I took the mobile phone. I needed to keep in touch.
I took the mobile phone to keep in touch.

1 I stayed at home. I had to do my homework.
2 My mother went into town. She wanted to do some shopping.
3 I bought a notepad so that I could write some letters.
4 I'm saving all my money because I want to buy a bike.
5 You need an extra sweater. You need to keep warm.

4 Choose the correct word.

I went to bed early ... I was tired out.
a) so b) because c) then

1 He wanted to know ... I told him the truth.
   a) then b) therefore c) so
2 I last went to the cinema three months ... .
   a) ago b) later c) since
3 I'm going to tidy my room ... breakfast.
   a) to b) after c) by
4 He never arrived so .... we left.
   a) after b) lastly c) in the end
5 ... I want to thank you for coming.
   a) First of all b) At first c) The first

Vocabulary

5 Complete the sentences with the correct word.

Road is to car as rail is to train.

1 Jazz is to music as football is to ... .
2 Guitar is to guitarist as drum is to ... .
3 Father is to son as mother is to ... .
4 Husband is to wife as uncle is to ... .
5 School is to pupil as college is to ... .
6 Second is to minute as minute is to ... .
7 Day is to week as month is to ... .

6 Sort the time adverbials into groups according to the form of the present tense with which they are usually used.

• always • now • currently • never • now and again
• often • at the moment • on Thursdays
• for the time being • every day

Present continuous	Present simple
now	*always*

Communication

7 Work in pairs. Student A ask Student B:

• how many brothers and sisters he/she has got.
• what subjects he/she likes doing at school.
• what he/she usually does in the evening to relax.
• what he/she did after school yesterday.
• how he/she spent last weekend.

Now Student B ask Student A:

• if he/she has got any pets at home.
• what sports he/she likes doing or watching.
• what he/she usually does to get up in time for school.
• what he/she did last night.
• how he/she spent last summer holidays.

Progress update Units 1 and 2

How do you rate your progress? Tick the chart.

	Excellent ★★★★	Good ★★★	OK ★★	Can do better ★
Grammar				
Vocabulary				
Communication				

3 A place which attracts tourists.

Cornwall

Learning goals

Communication
Talk about the future
Give and respond to invitations

Grammar
Defining and non-defining relative clauses with *who*, *which*, *where*
Future with *going to*, *will* or present continuous

Vocabulary
The natural environment

Cornwall, in the south-west of England, is a place which attracts tourists all the year round. It has mild weather and a spectacular coastline with beautiful bays and coves.

Not surprisingly, there are a hundred and one things for tourists to do in Cornwall. Seaside resorts like Newquay, which have wide, clean beaches, are very popular with families and also with people who like water sports, especially windsurfing and surfing. Land's End - the famous 'last place' in mainland Britain - has restaurants, amusements and wonderful coastal views. People who prefer to get away from the crowds can visit one of the many fishing villages along the coast, watch the seals at Cornwall's Seal Sanctuary or go inland onto the moors where the scenery is much wilder.

History lovers will enjoy seeing the village and ruined castle of Tintagel, where they can learn about Camelot and the legend of King Arthur. Or they can visit Poldhu Cove near Mullion, where Marconi, the Italian inventor, sent the first wireless signal across the Atlantic to Canada in 1901.

Cornwall has plenty to offer those who are interested in art and literature. Many artists and writers have lived and worked there. Famous names include the sculptor Barbara Hepworth, who had her studio in St Ives, the writer Daphne du Maurier, who wrote the best-selling novels *Rebecca* and *Jamaica Inn*, and the poet John Betjeman. Also in St Ives there is a branch of the famous art gallery, the Tate.

Like many beautiful places in the world there is another side to Cornwall, which visitors do not always see. Cornwall is quite isolated and, apart from tourism, there is not a lot of work for local people. Mining and fishing, which were once major industries, have almost disappeared and there is a high level of unemployment. The result is that many young Cornish people move away to places where they are more likely to find jobs.

Cornwall may sound like a tourists' paradise, but local people know that life can be hard when the visitors leave.

1 ⟩ Vocabulary

The natural environment

- beach • forest • mountain
- rock • valley • hill • cliff(s)
- bay • tree • coast/coastline
- cove • field • river • island
- moor • cave • lake • sea

a⟩ Sort the words into three categories. Words that:

1 are connected with water.
2 are connected with land.
3 combine water and land.

Look up any words you don't know.

b⟩ List any other words you know to describe the natural environment.

2 ⟩ Read

a⟩ Read the text about Cornwall and put these topic headings in the correct order.

2 a) holiday attractions
4 b) problems
3 c) cultural information
1 d) location and climate
2 e) places of historical interest

b⟩ Say where these people might like to go in Cornwall.

1 a wildlife enthusiast
2 a surfer
3 an artist
4 someone who is interested in history
5 someone who is interested in telecommunications

c⟩ Where would you like to go in Cornwall? Why?

Grammar flash

Defining and non-defining relative clauses with *who, which, where*

Read the text about Cornwall again and complete the rules.

1 Who, which *or* where?

- We use ... to describe people, ... to describe things and ... to describe places.

2 Defining or non-defining?

- ... relative clauses give essential information and do not have commas.
- ... relative clauses give additional information which can be omitted, and have commas before or on either side of the clause.

3 ⟩ Practice

Complete the sentences with the relative pronoun *who, which* **or** *where.* **Which sentences are D (defining) and which are ND (non-defining)?**

1 People who visit Cornwall return frequently. (D)

1 People ... visit Cornwall return frequently.
2 We visited the village of Polperro, ... was once a busy fishing centre.
3 You can see the exact place ... the first wireless signal was sent across the Atlantic to Canada.
4 South-west England is a region ... attracts visitors all the year round.
5 The writer Daphne du Maurier, ... wrote a short story called *The Birds*, lived near Fowey.
6 The Scilly Isles, ... the climate is mild all the year, are well worth a visit.

4 Listen and read

Nicola: Hi, Louise. How are things?

Louise: Fine, thanks. When are you starting work?

Nicola: This evening. I'm going to work in reception to start with. But I've got this afternoon free. Are you doing anything special?

Louise: No, not really.

Nicola: Do you fancy going for a bike ride?

Louise: Yes, OK. Good idea!

Nicola: Perhaps we could go and watch the surfers. Auntie Lynn, we're going off for the afternoon.

Lynn: That's nice. It's a lovely day. Are you going to walk?

Nicola: No, we're going to cycle. We'd like to borrow some bikes, if that's all right.

Lynn: Yes, of course. But don't forget that we're meeting at six o'clock this evening to talk about your work, Nicola.

Nicola: OK, I'll be back by six, I promise!

Lynn: All right. Have a nice time!

5 Comprehension

Correct the sentences.

1 No, she isn't. She's starting work this evening.

1 Nicola is starting work next week.
2 Louise is busy this afternoon.
3 Nicola and Louise are going to walk into town.
4 They have got their own bikes.
5 Nicola is meeting her aunt at seven o'clock.

6 Useful phrases

Listen and repeat.

- How are things?
- Fine, thanks.
- [...] to start with.
- No, not really.
- Good idea!
- [...], if that's all right.
- Yes, of course.
- Have a nice time!

Grammar snapshot

Future with *going to, will* **or present continuous**

a> Look at the sentences below and identify the three forms of the future.

1 We're **having** supper at six thirty.
2 We're **going to** walk along the cliffs.
3 I'**ll** be here at six.
4 I promise I **won't** be late.
5 I'll have an orange juice, please.

b> Make rules using *going to, will* or the present continuous.

1 We use ... to talk about future arrangements and plans which are already fixed. A time adverbial, e.g. *tomorrow, at midnight* is often used with this tense.
2 We use the ... future to talk about intentions.
3 We use ... for predictions, promises and decisions.

c> What's the difference in meaning?

1 I'**m going to see** him this evening.
2 I'**ll see** him this evening.
3 I'**m seeing** him this evening.

7> Practice

a> Write a sentence for each picture, using the correct form of *going to*.

1 'I'm going to watch some videos.'

1) I

2) they

3) she

4) he

b> Complete the dialogue with the present continuous or *will/won't*.

Nicola: What (you/do) ¹... next Tuesday?
Louise: I don't know. I expect I (be) ²... free. Why?
Nicola: Well, the Newquay Surf Club (do) ³... a display.
Louise: (you go) ⁴... to it?
Nicola: Yes, if I'm not working. Do you fancy coming?
Louise: Maybe. Where (they/have) ⁵... it?
Nicola: On Fistral Beach. I hope the South African surfing team (be) ⁶... there.
Louise: Why?
Nicola: I met one of them yesterday. I (tell) ⁷... you about him later.

8> ⦂⦂ Soundbite

Falling intonation on *Wh-* questions

What are you doing on Saturday?
(Look at page 122.)

9> Communication

Giving and responding to invitations

▶ What are you doing at the weekend?
▶ I'm seeing my cousins on Friday evening.
▶ Are you free on Saturday evening?
▶ Yes, I am./I don't know yet.
▶ Well, I'm going to see *Titanic*. Would you like to come?/Do you fancy coming?
▶ Yes, that would be great./Yes, OK. Good idea!/I'm not sure. Can I let you know?
▶ I'll phone you on Saturday morning.

Use the cues below to discuss dates with someone in your class. Then continue the conversation.

Student A: Activities on Friday
1 play in a volleyball match
2 look after my younger brother
3 revise for my Maths exam

Student B: Suggestions for Saturday
1 go tenpin bowling
2 see the new Will Smith film
3 try to get tickets for the Eternal concert

10 ▷ Read

Read the article and complete the chart.

Elena
Nationality:
Holiday destination:
Accommodation:
General activities:
Special event:

Elena, aged 15, from Sofia, Bulgaria

'This summer I'm not really having a holiday. I'm going to Russia with my gym club. I'm going to spend three weeks in Moscow training with Russian gymnasts and living with a Russian family. I'm looking forward to it but I'm a bit worried that I won't like the food. The Moscow gym club members are taking us to see the famous Bolshoi Ballet. They're performing *Swan Lake*, so that will be fun.'

11 ▷ 👄 Listen

Listen to Catherine talking about her holiday plans and answer the questions.

1 What sort of holiday does she hate?
2 Where is she going?
3 What is she going to do while she is there?

12 ▷ Writing helpline

Collect and organise ideas

Before writing a composition, it is important to organise your ideas. One way to do this is an ideas web. First, note down the main topics and number them in the best order. Then make a web, with the title in the centre, the main topic areas branching from it, and further branches from them for more details.

Copy the ideas web and complete it for yourself about your next, or an ideal, holiday.

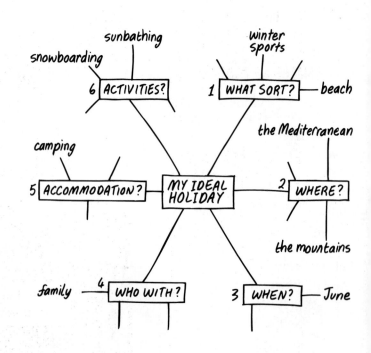

snowboarding
sunbathing
6 ACTIVITIES?
camping
5 ACCOMMODATION?
family — 4 WHO WITH?
MY IDEAL HOLIDAY
winter sports
1 WHAT SORT? — beach
the Mediterranean
2 WHERE?
the mountains
3 WHEN? — June

13 ▷ Write

Write about your plans for your next (real or imaginary) holiday. Use your ideas web to help you.

In town

Read the story and try to guess the missing words. Then listen and see if you were right.

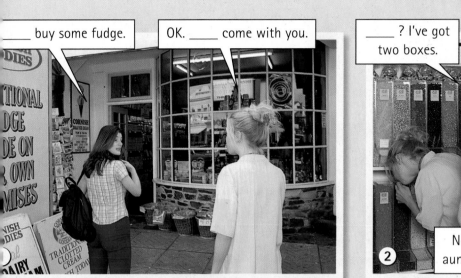

_____ buy some fudge.

OK. _____ come with you.

_____ ? I've got two boxes.

They're one pound eighty-five each. That's three pounds seventy altogether.

_____ holiday?

No, I'm going to work at my aunt's hotel. _____ this evening.

2

Don't forget your fudge!

_____ . Silly me!

_____ Tom. The boy who works at the hotel.

So it is.

4

Hi, Tom!

Hello, you two. How are things? _____ a milkshake?

No, thanks. I'm afraid I must go. _____ my aunt at six.

5

I'll stay. _____ OK with you, Nicola?

Yeah, no problem! _____ later!

Here's my brother, Jamie. Hi, Jamie!

That's odd, he doesn't usually want me around!

Hi, Tom! Can I come home with you?

Sure.

7

8

25

How long have you been here?

Learning goals

Communication
Ask and talk about experiences
Make comparisons

Grammar
Present perfect simple with *for* and *since*
Comparison of adjectives
Intensifier *much* + comparative adjective
Comparison with *(not) as … as*

Vocabulary
Adjectives with negative prefixes: *un-, in-, im-*

Born to

SALLY MARKS meets the surf addicts

It doesn't matter if the weather's good or bad, the real surf addicts are always out riding the waves.

Surfing is one of the world's most popular water sports. It has spread from the islands of Hawaii, where it originated, to beaches all over the world.

Newquay is the surfing capital of the UK. It is not as sunny or as hot as Bondi Beach in Australia or the beaches of southern California, but to the thousands of surfers who come here, it is 'Surf City' – the coolest place to be in Britain. Surfing has been one of the most important parts of Newquay's economy since the early 1990s. Every year it attracts more and more young people. Today there are thirty surf shops in the town.

In Newquay, there is a big difference between serious surfers and the so-called 'beach boys'. Serious surfers are much stronger, thinner and fitter than beach boys. They live to surf and nothing gets in their way. They surf three times a day if possible, in winter and in summer, and they never seem to notice the cold.

A typical serious surfer is 21-year-old Flip (nobody knows his real name). He gave up his job in a supermarket in London two years ago and has been in Cornwall ever since. Flip works as a part-time assistant in a surf shop in the morning and as a barman in a hotel at night. He has not had a night off for seven weeks but says: 'I'm not unhappy, because the jobs leave my afternoons free for surfing. I know I haven't got a career but I can't stop surfing. I expect that one day my lifestyle will be impractical and I'll have to find a full-time job. But at the moment I'm happy.'

surfing factfile

Where: Australia, France, Indonesia, Morocco, Portugal, Southern Ireland, UK (Cornwall), USA (California and Hawaii)

Famous beaches: Bondi (Australia), Fistral (UK), Malibu (USA), Waikiki (Hawaii – USA)

Scoring: Points for length of ride, control of board, style and confidence, choice of wave, timing

Essential equipment

for surfing: board, wetsuit, boots, leash, board bag

for après-surf: T-shirt, shorts, trainers, sunglasses, watch, suntan

Language:

radical	simply the best
a *tube*	a tunnel of moving water
a *wipeout*	a fall off your surfboard in the middle of a ride

---

Before you read

Have you ever done any surfing?
If not, would you like to try?

1 › Read

a › Read the article and answer the questions.

1 Where did surfing start?
2 When did surfing become important in Newquay?
3 What are the main differences between a serious surfer and a 'beach boy'?
4 How does Flip earn enough money to surf?

b › Guess the meaning of these phrases.

- the surfing capital   • to live to surf
- to get in someone's way   • to give up
- to have a night off

2 › Vocabulary

Adjectives with negative prefixes

- popular • happy • dependent • healthy
- practical • usual • formal • fashionable
- correct • important • possible • interesting
- pleasant • mature • comfortable • successful

To form the opposite meaning of each of the adjectives above we, use the prefixes *un-*, *in-* or *im-*.

List the adjectives under the correct prefix.

un-	in-	im-
unpopular	*independent*	*impractical*

3 › ⚬⚬ Sound bite

Word stress in adjectives

<u>pop</u>ular   un<u>pop</u>ular   (Look at page 122.)

4 › Practice

Complete the sentences with one of the adjectives from Exercise 2 with its negative prefix.

1 The film was very unpopular. Nobody went to see it.

1 The film was very ... . Nobody went to see it.
2 People don't eat a big fried breakfast any more because it's ... .
3 This crossword is ... . I can't solve any of the clues.
4 The book looked rather ... so I didn't buy it.
5 Jam and cheese is an ... combination but I love it.
6 Don't be so ... . You behave like a three-year-old sometimes.

ride

5 > 🔊 Listen and read

Nicola: Hello, Jake! Do you remember me – Nicola?

Jake: Sure I do!

Nicola: These are some friends from the hotel, Louise and Tom.

Tom: Hi! What's the surfing like today?

Jake: The waves are great. They're much better than yesterday.

Tom: How long have you been here in Newquay?

Jake: Since last Friday. I arrived the same day as Nicola.

Louise: How do you like it?

Jake: It's OK but it's not as lively as Cape Town! Have you ever been to South Africa?

Tom: No, never. Is the surfing good?

Jake: You bet. It's got the best surfing beaches you've ever seen!

Nicola: Are the beaches better than the ones in Hawaii?

Jake: Yes, absolutely. Have any of you ever been to Hawaii?

Tom: No.

Jake: It's radical. The waves are the highest in the world, and ...

Tom: Really? How wonderful! Does anyone fancy a hot dog?

6 > Comprehension

Answer T (true), F (false) or DK (don't know).

1 Jake is enjoying the surfing today.
2 He came to the beach early in the morning.
3 Jake has been in Cornwall longer than Nicola.
4 He has also surfed in Hawaii.
5 Tom likes Jake.

7 > 🔊 Useful phrases

Listen and repeat.

- Sure I do!
- What's [the surfing] like?
- No, never.
- You bet.
- Does anyone fancy [a hot dog]?

Grammar flash

Present perfect simple with *for* **and** *since*

How long have you been here?
– I've been here **for** a week.
– I've been here **since** Friday/June/ ten o'clock.

Make a rule.

When we use the present perfect simple tense, we use ... to talk about a period of time and ... to talk about a point in time.

8 Practice

a) List the time expressions under two headings: those which take *for* **and those which take** *since*.

• three days • a year • July • six months
• last Wednesday • days and days • 1989
• he was a child • May 25th • four weeks
• I started school • I was born • a short time

b) Make sentences using the present perfect of the verb in brackets with *for* **or** *since*.

1 Louise has been a vegetarian since 1997.

1 Louise became a vegetarian in 1997. (be)
2 The Tremaynes moved to Newquay when they were married. (live)
3 Nicola gave up sweets two years ago. (not eat)
4 Jake learnt to surf when he was eight. (know)

c) Make similar sentences of your own.

9 Communication

Asking and talking about experiences

▶ How long have you been at this school?
▶ I've been here for/since ... .
▶ Have you ever wanted to change schools?
▶ No, because all my friends are here.

a) Use the cues to have similar conversations. Note your partner's answers.

1 know/best friend//ever go on holiday together?
2 live/ in *(town)*//ever want to live in another town?
3 have/your favourite pair of jeans//ever buy an expensive pair of trousers?

b) Tell the class about your partner.

Giovanni has been at this school ... .

Grammar snapshot

Comparison of adjectives

Comparative
The waves are **better** today **than** yesterday.
The town is **more** crowd**ed** today **than** yesterday.

Superlative
Cornwall has got some of **the** clean**est** beaches you've ever seen!
Cape Town is one of **the most spectacular** cities in the world.

Comparison with *much* **plus comparative**
The town is **much noisier/much more crowded** today **than** yesterday.

Comparison with *(not) as ... as ...*
Cornwall is**n't as** hot **as** Hawaii.
The waves in Australia are **as** big **as** the waves in South Africa.

Make rules.

1 How do we make the comparative and superlative forms of adjectives?
2 Which word can we use to make a comparative stronger?
3 Which words do we use to say things are the same?

10 Practice

Complete the sentences with *much* **or** *as ... as* **and the correct form of the adjective in brackets.**

1 Toledo in Spain is ... than Newquay. (beautiful)
2 Is the population of India ... that of China? (large)
3 The beaches on the Costa Blanca are ... than the beaches on the Costa Brava. (long)
4 The shops here aren't ... in the capital. (fashionable)
5 The weather is ... than it was last year. (good)

11 Listen

Listen to a surfer and answer the questions.

1 Which three beaches does he compare?
2 How does he compare:
   a) the waves?   b) the temperature?
3 What sort of accidents can happen?
4 Where is he going next?

The world about us
What do you know? What do you think?

Topics

1 Animals 2 People 3 Inventions 4 Buildings
5 Cities 6 Countries 7 Film stars 8 Historical events

Adjectives

- endangered • important • interesting • famous
- expensive • popular • successful • beautiful
- powerful • useful • crowded • polluted • ugly
- big • fast • slow

12 > Over to you

a) Make a quiz about the world today. Choose topics and adjectives from the box above (or think of your own) and write ten questions like these.

1 *Which animal is more endangered – the gorilla or the African elephant?*
2 *Who is the most powerful person in the world?*
3 *Is a Harley Davidson motorbike more expensive than a BMW car?*

b) In pairs, ask and answer the questions. Note your partner's answers and tell the class.

Juliet says that the gorilla is much more endangered than the African elephant.
She thinks that the President of the USA is the most powerful person in the world.

13 > Writing helpline

Express opinions

When writing a composition, it is useful to distinguish between fact and opinion. When you give an opinion, you can use phrases like:

I (definitely) think that ...
In my opinion, ...

14 > Write

Write answers to three of the questions you talked about in Exercise 12.

In my opinion, the three most famous people in the world today are ...

Fast rewind UNITS 3 and 4

Grammar

1 Complete the conversation during a walking holiday with the correct form of the *going to* or the *will* future.

A: When (we/stop) [1] *are we going to stop?*
B: We (take a break) [2] ... soon, I promise. You (not/be) [3] ... in a bad mood all afternoon, are you?
A: No, I (feel better) [4] ... after a rest.
B: We can't stop now. I think it (rain) [5] ... in a minute.
A: When we get to the hostel I (have) [6] ... a long hot shower and go to bed!

2 Make sentences in the present perfect simple tense with *for* or *since*.

I/not be/to the dentist/two years.
I haven't been to the dentist for two years.

1 I/know my friend Paul/1997.
2 My sister/be/in hospital/several weeks.
3 he/wear glasses/a long time?
4 She/not live/at home/February.
5 I/not see/my cousin/last summer.

3 Complete the sentences with *who, which* and *where*.

Can I speak to someone *who* works here?

1 Have you got a book ... describes the wildlife in Cornwall?
2 Wembley Arena is ... they have a lot of pop concerts.
3 My brother, ... is living abroad, has just got engaged.
4 Do you know a place near here ... I can change money?
5 They sat at a desk ... was near the back of the room.
6 How many people do you know ... have mobile phones?

4 Complete the comparisons using the adjectives in brackets.

London is *more expensive* now than Paris. (expensive)

1 Windsurfing is ... than waterskiing. (exciting)
2 Which is ... city in your country? (beautiful)
3 His jokes are much ... than yours. (bad)
4 The ... place in the world is in Hawaii. (wet)
5 The Matterhorn is not ... as Mount Everest. (high)
6 When is ... time of year to visit Florida? (good)
7 The ... places on earth are in Antarctica. (dry)
8 The violin is ... to play than the guitar. (difficult)
9 Bath is not ... from London as Bristol. (far)
10 This is ... book about Cornwall I've ever read. (interesting)

Vocabulary

5 Complete the sentences with the correct word.

1 The longest ... in the world is the Nile.
2 The Seychelles are a group of ... in the Indian Ocean.
3 The Pyrenees are ... between Spain and France.
4 Most of Finland consists of forests and ... .
5 Tropical rain ... are rapidly disappearing.

6 Complete the sentences with the negative form of the most suitable adjective.

• practical • important • formal • dependent
• fashionable • popular • pleasant

I threw away the letter. It was *unimportant*.

1 She gave away some clothes because they were ... .
2 My brother is so ... ! He can't even boil an egg.
3 The party will be very .... so you can wear jeans.
4 She doesn't want to live at home. She wants to be ... .
5 He's ... at work because he says ... things to people.

Communication

7 Work in pairs. Student A ask Student B:

• what he/she is doing tomorrow evening.
• if he/she has ever seen Janet Jackson in real life.
• if he/she would like to go to see her in concert.
• for his/her telephone number at home.
Say when you will phone him/her to fix a time to meet.

Now Student B ask Student A:

• what he/she is doing next weekend.
• if he/she has ever slept in a tent.
• if he/she would like to go camping with you in the country.
• for his/her telephone number at home.
Say when you will phone him/her to make arrangements.

Progress update Units 3 and 4

How do you rate your progress? Tick the chart.

	Excellent ★★★★	Good ★★★	OK ★★	Can do better ★
Grammar				
Vocabulary				
Communication				

SOUTH AFRICA

NEW DEMOCRACY

South Africa has been a democracy since 1994, when the apartheid system came to an end and it held its first democratic elections. Apartheid* (separate development), which began in 1948, was one of the most inhumane systems of government in history. It did not allow black people to mix with white people at school, at college, at work, in marriage, on public transport or even on park benches.

*Apartheid is pronounced / əˈpɑːteɪt /

CITY OF DURBAN
UNDER SECTION 37 OF THE DURBAN BEACH BY-LAWS, THIS BATHING AREA IS RESERVED FOR THE SOLE USE OF MEMBERS OF THE WHITE RACE GROUP.

STAD DURBAN
HIERDIE GEBIED IS, INGEVOLGE ARTIKEL 37 VAN DIE DURBANSE STRANDVERORDENINGE, UITGEHOU VIR DIE UITSLUITLIKE GEBRUIK VAN LEDE VAN DIE BLANKE RASSEGROEP.

LANDSCAPE AND WILDLIFE

With its high mountains and cliffs, sandy beaches, dense forests and huge deserts, South Africa has one of the most varied landscapes in the world.

Wildlife is a major tourist attraction. It's the best place in the world to see the 'Big Five': lion, leopard, buffalo, elephant and rhino. Most animals live in huge game reserves like the Kruger National Park, where they are safe from hunters.

The sealife is also rich and varied. Along the rocky Atlantic coast near Cape Town you can see seals and penguins, and at False Bay, which is a favourite place for whales and their young, many people go whale-watching during October and November.

NELSON MANDELA

Nelson Mandela founded the African National Congress (ANC) Youth League in 1944 and fought apartheid for all his early life. In 1962 he went to prison for life. Twenty years later, in 1982, a huge 'Release Mandela' campaign started. He finally left prison in 1990, after nearly twenty-eight years. In 1994 he became the first elected black leader of the South African people.

Before you read

Write three things you know and three things you want to know about South Africa.

1> Read

a> Read the text and note what happened on each of these key dates in South Africa's history.

1 1944   2 1948   3 1962   4 1982   5 1990   6 1994

b> Answer the questions.

1 What was the basic principle of apartheid?
2 What was special about Mandela's election?
3 What is dramatic about the view in Cape Town?
4 What are the 'Big Five' and where can you see them in South Africa?
5 What is special about False Bay?

2> 👁 Listen

Listen to Zola talking about his daily life at school in Cape Province. What does he say about:

1 how he helps his mother?   4 his school hours?
2 his class?   5 his father?
3 his teacher?   6 his free-time activities?

3> Write

Imagine you are going on a tour of South Africa. Write a letter to a penfriend about what you are going to see and do while you are there.

4> Discussion

Do you think that racism still exists in South Africa? Where else does it exist? Do you think only older people are racist?

Try to use these expressions in your discussion.

I think/don't think that ...
In my opinion, ...
I agree/I don't agree.
I see what you mean, but ...

5> Speak and write

You are going to design an Internet website about your country. Discuss the information you would include. Then write the details.

SOUTH AFRICA FACTFILE

Population: 37.9 million
Black Africans: (76.1%)
White: (13.1%)
Asians: (13%)
Coloured (people of mixed descent) (8.5%)

Languages: There are now eleven official languages, including English.

Capital cities: Cape Town (legislative)
Pretoria (administrative)
Bloemfontein (judicial)

Main exports: Gold, diamonds, other minerals, fruit, vegetables, tobacco, textiles

A ▶ A beautiful place in your country

Write an article about an area of outstanding natural beauty in your country and find pictures to illustrate it. Imagine you are visiting the area.

Say why the area is important.

This week we are visiting Snowdonia National Park in North Wales. This is a region of mountains which includes Mount Snowdon, the second highest mountain in Britain. It is

Say what the scenery is like.

The scenery in Snowdonia is very dramatic with high mountains and

Say what you did yesterday.

Yesterday we stayed at a youth hostel on the shores of a beautiful lake. In the morning we went walking. Then

Say what you are going to do tomorrow.

Tomorrow we are going to travel on the famous Llanberis mountain railway. This is a small, single track railway which carries visitors to the top of Mount Snowdon. In the afternoon we

B ▶ A beautiful place in another country

Imagine you are visiting an area of outstanding beauty in another country. Find out about the area, collect pictures and write about it. Choose one of the following places, or write about an area of your own choice.

- the Valley of the Kings in Egypt
- the Himalayas in Nepal
- the Sahara Desert in North Africa
- the Great Barrier Reef in Australia

CALIFORNIA GIRLS

Well, east coast girls are hip.
I really dig those styles ¹............ .
And the ²............ girls with the way they talk,
They knock me out when I'm down there.

The mid-west ³............ daughters
Really make you ⁴............ .
And the northern girls with the way they kiss,
They keep their boyfriends warm ⁵............ .

Chorus
I wish they all could be Californian,
I wish they all could be Californian,
I wish they all could be California girls!

The west ⁶............ has the sunshine
And ⁷............ all get so tanned
I dig a French bikini on Hawaiian island dolls
By a palm tree ⁸............ .

I've been all around ⁹............
And ¹⁰............ all kind of girls
Yes, but I couldn't wait ¹¹............ in the States,
Back to the cutest girls ¹²............ .

Repeat chorus twice

California Girls was one of the most successful songs of the American group The Beach Boys. In the 1960s this and other songs about surfing and beach life in southern California, such as *Surfing USA* and *Good Vibrations*, became very popular.

1▷ 👀 Read the lyrics of the song and guess which of these words and phrases fits each gap. Then listen and see if you were right.

- coast • farmers' • the girls • southern
- this great big world • in the sand
- in the world • to get back • feel all right
- at night • I've seen • they wear

2▷ Which parts of the USA do all the girls who are mentioned in the song come from?

3▷ Which colloquial words and expressions in the first verse mean the same as the following?

1 cool and modern   3 fashions
2 like very much   4 impress

6 The car was sinking.

Learning goals

Communication
Talk about past incidents
Ask for and give directions

Grammar
Past simple and continuous
Time markers: *while, as, when*
Prepositions of motion: *across, along, from, towards, through, past, into, over, under, up, down*

Vocabulary
Verbs of movement: *dive, jump, leap*, etc.

SCUBA HERO RESCUES DROWNING MOTORIST

A SCUBA DIVER rescued a 37-year-old motorist from her car, which was 20ft under water, after she accidentally drove into a marina yesterday.

Mother-of-two Mrs Chorpa was trying to help her father-in-law to start his car with some jump leads from the engine of her own car. While she was sitting in her car, she accidentally put it in gear and the car suddenly leapt forward over the edge of the marina. It fell onto a wooden jetty and then bounced into the water.

Two boat repairers, Jim Fry and Rod Jenkins, who were standing nearby, saw the accident. They immediately dived in and tried to free the woman from the car. Mr Jenkins said: 'The car was slowly sinking. We tried to get Mrs Chorpa to open the car door but she couldn't. She just held on to the steering wheel.'

Fortunately yachtsman Stuart Bowen-Davies, an experienced scuba diver, saw the accident and jumped into the water with his scuba gear. 'I was on my boat getting ready to go on a dive, when suddenly I saw what was happening.' Stuart swam towards the car, which was sinking fast, got to the woman through an open window and gave her some air from his scuba tank. 'As she was breathing in some air, I managed to pull her out through the window and up to the surface. My main worry was that we were too late.'

Back on land, Stuart gave Mrs Chorpa mouth-to-mouth resuscitation. She is now recovering in hospital.

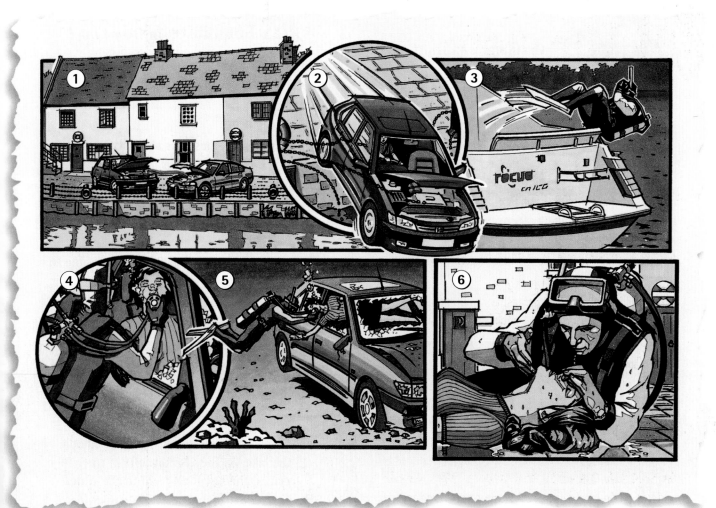

1 Read

a Read the newspaper article and match each caption with the correct picture.

Picture 1c) Mrs Chorpa helps to start her father-in-law's car with jump leads.

a) A scuba diver dives into the marina with scuba equipment.

b) The diver gives the woman mouth-to-mouth resuscitation.

c) Mrs Chorpa helps to start her father-in-law's car with jump leads.

d) The diver gives the woman some air.

e) Mrs Chorpa accidentally puts the car into gear and the car falls into the marina.

f) The diver pulls the woman through the car window.

b Find words in the article which mean the same as the following.

• by mistake • side • equipment
• was able to • top of the water
• getting better

2 Vocabulary

Verbs of movement

• leap • fall • bounce • dive • sink • jump • swim

Look at the verbs above and notice how they are used in the article.

3 Practice

Complete the sentences with the verbs of movement from Exercise 2 in the past simple tense.

1 The boat had a hole in it and it sank to the bottom of the sea.

1 The boat had a hole in it and it ... to the bottom of the sea.

2 He didn't want to dive so he ... into the water instead.

3 She ... beautifully from the high board.

4 He threw the ball down hard and it ... high into the air.

5 The little girl dropped her doll and it ... into the water.

6 When they got home their dog ... up happily to greet them.

7 We ... across the river to the island.

Grammar snapshot

Past simple and continuous

a Look at the sentences below. Which verbs are in the past continuous and which are in the past simple?

1 I **stayed** in a hotel in Cornwall last summer.
2 While/As I **was working** on the boat, I **saw** someone fall in.
3 I **was working** on my boat when I **saw** the accident in the marina.

b Go back and look.
Find examples of the past continuous tense in the newspaper article in Exercise 1.

c Make rules.
Past simple or past continuous?

1 We use the ... tense to talk about past events which are finished or completed.
2 We use the ... tense to describe events which were happening over a period of time in the past.
3 Clauses in the ... tense are often introduced by *while* or *as*.
4 Clauses in the ... tense are often introduced by *when*.

d What's the difference in meaning?
1 When I saw him, he **was making** a phone call.
2 When I saw him, he **made** a phone call.

4 Soundbite The sound / ɪŋ /

work**ing** wait**ing** hav**ing** (Look at page 122.)

5 Practice

a Answer the questions about the rescue using the past continuous.

1 What was Mrs Chorpa doing at the time of the accident?
2 Where was she when the car suddenly moved forward?
3 Why were Jim Fry and Rod Jenkins able to act so quickly?
4 What was the yachtsman doing at the time?
5 What was happening to the car?

b Use the cues to complete the conversation using the past continuous or the past simple.

A: Guess what happened while we (swim) [1] *were swimming* in the lake yesterday afternoon!
B: What?
A: A boy and a girl (row) [2] ... in the middle of the lake. As they (stand up) [3] ... to change places, the boy (fall) [4] ... into the water.
B: Then what (happen) [5] ... ?
A: A lifeguard, who (watch) [6] ... everybody, (see) [7] ... what happened.
B: What (do) [8] ... he ... ?
A: He (jump) [9] ... into the water and (rescue) [10] ... the boy.

c⟩ Make a similar conversation using the pictures on the right and the cues below.

1 shop/for clothes/department store
2 wait to pay/man steal my purse
3 security guard/watch on closed circuit TV/see everything
4 arrest/leave the store

6⟩ Over to you

How good is your memory? Ask and answer the questions.

1 What were you wearing yesterday?
2 What were you doing at eight o'clock last night?
3 Which book were you using in English this time last year?
4 What were you studying in History last term?
5 What was in fashion last year? What sort of clothes were people wearing?

7⟩ 😊 Listen

Listen to Matthew talking about an incident that happened last year and answer the questions.

1 What was Matthew doing at the time?
2 What did he and his friend see?
3 What did Matthew and his friend do?
4 What happened then?
5 What caused the incident in the first place?

8⟩ Write

Write at least three paragraphs about an incident. Either imagine that you saw the incident Matthew talks about in Exercise 7, or write about something that happened to you.

Write about:
• where you were and what you were doing at the time.
• how the incident happened.
• the result of the incident.

Grammar flash

Prepositions of motion
- into • towards • from • past
- through • across • along • up
- down • over • under

9 Practice

Complete the directions for a treasure hunt using a different preposition each time.

- Take the B3263 road ¹*from* Boscastle. You will come to Bossiney Castle mound on your left.
- Go ²*along* Bossiney Road until you see a bridge ³... the road. Walk ⁴... the bridge into the village of Tintagel.
- Walk ⁵... the village, ⁶... the Old Post Office until you see the gift shop.
- Go straight on and take the footpath on the left of the book shop, climbing ⁷... the hill ⁸... the cliffs.
- Look for some steps leading ⁹... to the beach.
- When the tide is out, walk ¹⁰... the sands to The Island. You will see Merlin's Cave in front of you.
- Walk ¹¹... the cave and look for the next clue.

10 Communication

Asking for and giving directions

▶ Excuse me,
could you tell me where the Old Post Office is?
could you tell me the way to the Old Post Office?
is there a post office near here?

▶ Yes, sure./Certainly.
Walk along this street as far as the bridge.
Go up/down this street until you get to the bridge.
Turn left/right.
Take the first/second turning on the left/right.

Ask for directions from:

1 the Old Post Office to Hole Beach.
2 the newsagent's to the playing fields.
3 the youth hostel to the pancake shop.
4 King Arthur's Great Halls to Bossiney Cove.

11 Write

Write the directions:

1 for the treasure hunt from Merlin's Cave to Bossiney Castle mound.

2 from your school to these places in your town:
a) a cinema   b) a sports shop   c) a bank

Looking for Jake

Read the story and put the pictures in the correct order. Then listen and see if you were right.

1 = Picture C

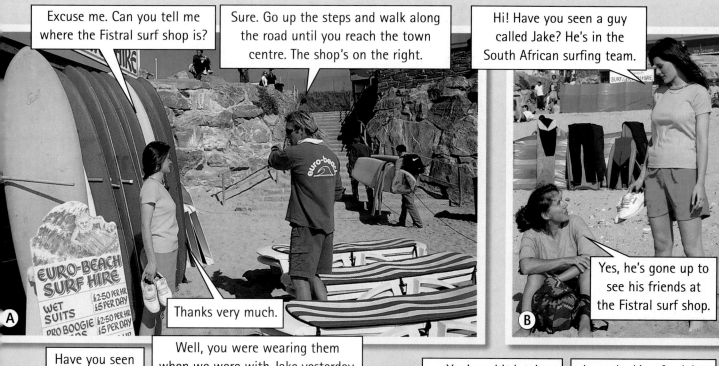

Excuse me. Can you tell me where the Fistral surf shop is?

Sure. Go up the steps and walk along the road until you reach the town centre. The shop's on the right.

Hi! Have you seen a guy called Jake? He's in the South African surfing team.

Thanks very much.

EURO-BEACH SURF HIRE
WET SUITS £2·50 PER HR £5 PER DAY
PRO BOOGIE £2·50 PER HR £5 PER DAY

Yes, he's gone up to see his friends at the Fistral surf shop.

A

B

Have you seen my sunglasses?

Well, you were wearing them when we were with Jake yesterday, and then you took them off.

C

You're a bit late! Where have you been?

I was looking for Jake, but I couldn't find him.

Hard luck!

D

Maybe Jake picked them up by mistake. I'll go and find him after work. Anyway, he promised to lend me a book about surfing.

Excuse me. Is Jake here?

He was here a moment ago. He was looking at our new surfboards. But then he went off.

Oh, never mind.

E

F

7 ▶ You're Nicola, aren't you?

Learning goals

Communication
Check information

Grammar
Question tags
Present perfect simple with
 time adverbials *just,
 already, yet*
Past simple and present
 perfect simple

Vocabulary
Clothes and parts of clothes
Humour

1 ▶ 👓 Listen and read

Tom: Hi, Nicola! This is your first morning in the restaurant, isn't it? How's it going?

Nicola: It's a disaster. I've already done something wrong!

Tom: What's the matter? What have you done?

Nicola: Look, I'm so clumsy! I've just spilt coffee on the sleeve of my blouse.

Tom: Have you seen Morris yet?

Nicola: No, I haven't. He's the deputy manager, isn't he?

Tom: Yes. He's quite fussy. You'd better go and change. Whoops! Too late! Here he is now!

Morris: Morning, everybody! Hello, you're Nicola, aren't you?

Nicola: Yes, that's right.

Morris: Have you worked in a restaurant before?

Nicola: No, I'm afraid I haven't.

Morris: Well, we all work very hard, don't we, Tom? Just a minute, Nicola. That isn't a stain on your blouse, is it?

Nicola: Yes, I'm sorry. It's only coffee.

Morris: Well, please go and change. I like my staff to look smart.

42

2 Comprehension

Answer T (true), F (false) or DK (don't know).

1 This is Nicola's first day at work in the restaurant.
2 Nicola is not in a very good mood.
3 She is wearing a clean white blouse.
4 Nicola wants to have some breakfast.
5 Morris doesn't notice that Nicola's blouse is dirty.

3 ⊙⊙ Useful phrases

Listen and repeat.

- How's it going?
- It's a disaster.
- What's the matter?
- Whoops!
- Too late!
- Here he is now!
- That's right.
- Just a minute.

4 Memory bank

Clothes and parts of clothes

a) List all the words to do with clothes that you can think of.

b) Say on which clothes you would find:

- sleeves • a hem • a collar
- turn-ups • cuffs • laces
- pockets

Grammar snapshot

Question tags

Positive statements with negative tags	Negative statements with positive tags
You're Nicola, **aren't** you?	That **isn't** a stain on your blouse, **is** it?
She's working in a hotel, **isn't** she?	They **don't** live in Newquay, **do** they?
We all **work** hard, **don't** we?	He **didn't** see us, **did** he?
He's got a holiday job, **hasn't** he?	
They **travelled** by train, **didn't** they?	

a) Make a rule.
To check information:
1 we use a *positive* statement followed by a ... tag (when we expect the answer 'Yes'.)
2 we use a *negative* statement followed by a ... tag (when we expect the answer 'No'.)

b) What's the difference in meaning?
1 You haven't been here before, have you?
2 You've been here before, haven't you?

5 ⊙⊙ Soundbite

Falling intonation with question tags

You're Nicola, aren't you?   It's cold, isn't it?   (Look at page 122.)

6 Practice

Complete the questions with the correct tags.

1 Your name's Jake, ... ?
2 They live in Newquay, ... ?
3 Nicola didn't have a good journey, ... ?
4 She's been travelling all night, ... ?
5 They've got a cousin in Florida, ... ?
6 You don't live here all the time, ... ?
7 He speaks English very well, ... ?
8 We're going to have a good time, ... ?

7 Communication

Checking information

▶ You're Nicola, aren't you?
▶ Yes, that's right.

Ask questions to check the information about your partner.

- his/her middle name • mother/father's job
- number of family members • pets • which hobbies he/she likes

Grammar snapshot

Present perfect simple with time adverbials *just, already, yet*

I've **just** spilt some coffee on my blouse.
I've **already** done something wrong.
Has Morris spoken to you **yet**?
He hasn't arrived **yet**.

Make rules.

With the present perfect simple tense:

1 the words *just* and *already* usually come ... the auxiliary verb and the main verb.
2 the word *yet* always comes at the ... of the sentence.
3 we normally use ... and ... in positive statements.
4 we normally use ... in negative statements and questions.

8 > Practice

a> In pairs, use the cues below and *What's ... like?* **to ask and answer questions. Use the present perfect with** *already* **in your answers.**

1 A: *What's the new sports stadium like?*
   B: *It's great! I've already swum there twice!*

1 the new sports stadium (swim/there/twice)
2 the new Spielberg film (see/with Jack)
3 the latest Boyzone album (listen to/three times)
4 Niko's café (be/there/to have coffee)
5 your new trainers (wear/to play tennis)
6 your new computer game (play/ten times)

b> Look at the pictures below and choose two related cues to make statements about them. Use the present perfect with *just* **and** *yet.*

• iron • dry her hair • get dressed • read
• write a letter • wake up • make a pizza
• put it in the oven • post • collect his fan mail
• wash the clothes • have a shower

1 *He's just woken up but he hasn't got dressed yet.*

⚡ Grammar flash

Past simple and present perfect simple

We **went** to Las Vegas last summer.
We **have** just **come back** from Rome.

Make a rule.

1 We use the ... tense to talk about an action in the past that is still of present interest.
2 We use the ... tense to talk about a completed action in the past.

Note

We can use past time adverbials like *ago, yesterday, last year, in 1989* with the past simple tense, but not with the present perfect tense.

I started two weeks ago.
not   X *I've started two weeks ago* X.

9 ⟩ Practice

Complete the conversation using the present perfect or the past simple tense of the verbs.

Dad: Hi, Ellie! Where (have/be) [1] *have you been*?
Ellie: I (be) [2] ... to the cinema with Katie.
        I (just/get back) [3] ... .
Dad: So, what film (you/see) [4] ...?
Ellie: We (see) [5] ... the new Will Smith film.
        (you/see) [6] ... it?
Dad: No, I haven't. But I (hear) [7] ... a lot about it.
        Anyway, (you both/enjoy) [8] ... it?
Ellie: Well, Katie (not]/like) [9] ... it but I (think) [10] ...
        it was great. Where's Mum?
Dad: She (already/go to bed) [11] ... . She (be) [12] ... a
        bit tired. But she (not/go to sleep/yet) [13] ... .
        She's reading.
Ellie: OK. I'll go and say goodnight to her. 'Night,
        Dad.
Dad: Goodnight, Ellie.

10 ⟩ Over to you

Talk about any new films, computer games and TV series that are popular at the moment.

A: *Have you seen (the new Jim Carrey film)?*
B: *No, I haven't. Have you?*
A: *Yes, I saw it at the weekend. It's great.*

11 ⟩ 👀 Listen

A radio interviewer stops a tourist family outside Buckingham Palace. Listen and note the places and musicals they have been to.

12 ⟩ Write

Imagine that you are visiting London or your capital city. Write a postcard to an English-speaking friend. Say what you have already seen or done, and what you haven't done yet.

What makes you laugh?

People in every part of the world have their own particular sense of humour. A Swedish joke is not necessarily funny in Saudi Arabia and a British joke isn't always funny in Japan. This is because many types of comedy, such as stand-up comedy, satire and TV 'sit-coms' (situation comedies) depend on individual national culture.

Slapstick and cartoons, however, are popular everywhere, because they are largely visual. The international success of Charlie Chaplin, Laurel and Hardy, Jim Carrey and cartoons like *The Simpsons* proves this.

Mr Bean is an example of how slapstick travels easily from one country to another. The first Mr Bean television programme appeared in the UK on New Year's Day in 1990. Eighteen million people watched it. Since then Mr Bean has been seen on TV in ninety-four countries, including Venezuela and Zimbabwe. The programmes have made Rowan Atkinson, the actor who plays Mr Bean, a millionaire.

John Porter talks to Rowan Atkinson about Mr Bean.

What is Mr Bean like?

In one way, Mr Bean's a very selfish character. The reason he gets into trouble is because he's quite clumsy and behaves badly and he doesn't care about anybody else. But in another way he's also sweet and innocent.

Are you similar to Mr Bean in any way?

No, not at all. I'm actually very slow and careful.

Do you know anybody like him?

No, I don't think anybody exists who is exactly like him. But there are people in life who seem to attract disaster and things go wrong for them all the time. Some people are naturally clumsy.

---

13 > Reading helpline

Use visual clues to help you read

Most reading texts have one or more of the following features: a title, a headline, a chapter heading or subheadings. Some also have pictures, photographs, diagrams or maps. All these visual clues help you to predict the content of the text.

Look at the title of the article, the pictures and the subheading and say what the article is about.

14 > Read

Read the article in detail and answer T (true), F (false) or DK (don't know).

1 People in different countries find different things funny.
2 Slapstick humour depends on a shared culture.
3 Charlie Chaplin has always been popular in many countries.
4 *Mr Bean* was not a success when it first appeared on British television.
5 *Mr Bean* has been shown in South Africa.
6 Rowan Atkinson is exactly like Mr Bean.

15 > Vocabulary

Humour

- sense of humour • joke
- stand-up comedy/comedian
- cartoon • slapstick • satire
- situation comedy (sit-com)

Which types of comedy do you prefer?

16 > Over to you

What do you and your friends find funny? In groups, make a survey to find the top three most popular:

- TV sit-coms.
- TV stand-up comedians.
- film comedies.

Fast rewind UNITS 6 and 7

Grammar

1〉 **Complete the text with the correct form of the verbs in brackets.**

A real life story

One day I (play) [1] *was playing* football with some friends, when I (see) [2] ... four boys on a bridge nearby. They (laugh) [3] ... and (shout) [4] ... and I (wonder) [5] ... what they (do) [6] ... . Then I (notice) [7] ... that they (wave) [8] ... a puppy in the air. When the boys (see) [9] ... me, they (throw) [10] ... the puppy over the bridge and it (fall) [11] ... into the river. They (run) [12] ... off laughing. I (jump) [13] ... over the wall, (run) [14] ... down to the river and (leap) [15] ... into the water. I (grab) [16] ... the puppy and (swim) [17] ... back to safety. My friends, who (stand) [18] ... on the bridge, (clap) [19] ... . I was a hero!

2〉 **Complete the conversation with the correct form of the verb and the time adverbials.**

1 Louise: Tom/go? (yet)   *Has Tom gone yet?*
2 Morris: Yes, he/stop work/about an hour. (ago)
3 Louise: Oh! he/finish for the day? (already)
4 Morris: Yes, he/cycle into town. (just)
5 Louise: he/leave/a message for me before he/go?
6 Morris: I don't know. you/ask/at the reception desk?
7 Louise: No/I/not/be there. (yet) Thanks.

3〉 **Complete the sentences with the correct question tag.**

You're Italian, ... ? *You're Italian, aren't you?*
1 Nicola isn't French, ... ?
2 Louise is staying at the hotel, ... ?
3 Tom wasn't at work yesterday, ... ?
4 Jake doesn't live in America, ... ?
5 You've been to Cornwall before, ... ?
6 Nicola can't play the piano, ... ?
7 There aren't any big rivers in Cornwall, ... ?

4〉 **Complete the sentences with a preposition of motion.**

With horror, he saw a train coming *towards* him.

1 We walked ... the bank of the river as far as the bridge.
2 We crossed ... the bridge to the road.
3 The children crawled ... the bed to hide.
4 It's hard to walk ... a hill, but it's easy to run ... it.
5 I pushed my way ... the thick jungle.
6 She told him to come away ... the edge of the cliff.
7 She dived ... the water and swam ... the river to the other side.

Vocabulary

5〉 **Match the parts of clothes with the most appropriate part of the body.**

1e) cuffs – wrist

1	cuffs	a)	foot
2	sleeves	b)	hip
3	turn-ups	c)	neck
4	hem	d)	arm
5	laces	e)	wrist
6	pockets	f)	knee
7	collar	g)	ankle

Communication

6〉 **Nicola sees someone she thinks she knows. Complete the question tags she uses to confirm the information.**

1 You're Mandy Brown, aren't you?

Nicola: You're Mandy Brown, [1] ... ?
Girl: Sorry?
Nicola: I'm Nicola. You remember me, [2] ... ?
Girl: I can't say I do.
Nicola: But you went to North Street Primary, [3] ... ?
Girl: No, I think you've got the wrong person.
Nicola: But you've got an older sister, [4] ... ?
Girl: Yes.
Nicola: And she's called Sally, [5] ... ?
Girl: No, my sister's name is Lara.
Nicola: Oh sorry! I've really made a fool of myself, [6] ... ?

Progress update Units 6 and 7

How do you rate your progress? Tick the chart.

	Excellent ★★★★	Good ★★★	OK ★★	Can do better ★
Grammar				
Vocabulary				
Communication				

8 ▷ You ought to try them.

Learning goals

Communication
Give advice
Talk about obligations
Make requests with reasons

Grammar
Verbs *should* and *ought to*
Verbs *have to* and *must/mustn't*
Would you mind ... ? + gerund

Vocabulary
Verbs connected with
food and cooking

1▷ 😐 Listen and read

Tom: Hi, Mum! We're going to have something to eat and watch a video. Is that OK?

June: Fine. Hello everyone. Would you mind getting your own meal? I have to go out.

Tom: No problem!

June: Oh, and Tom, could you give Jamie something to eat, too? He's watching TV.

Tom: OK. Bye, Mum!
Well, what do you fancy to eat? What about hot dogs? We can grill some sausages and we've got some rolls.

Nicola: Yum! Sounds great! Can I give you a hand?

Tom: Yes, OK. Could you turn the grill on?

Louise: No hot dogs for me, thanks.

Tom: But these sausages are really nice. You ought to try them.

Louise: No, thanks. I'm a vegetarian. I'll just have a cheese salad. Have you got any grated cheese?

Tom: Yes, I think so. You should eat more, Louise. You're too thin. Turn the grill up higher, Nicola.

Nicola: You shouldn't have it too hot. The sausages will burn.

Tom: Relax! I know what I'm doing. Let's go and watch TV.

A few minutes later

Jamie: I've got hiccups. I must get a glass of water. Hey! What's that smell?

Tom: Oh, no! The sausages have caught fire!

Nicola: Quick! Turn off the gas!

Tom: Pass me that tea towel!

Nicola: Well, Jamie, I hope you like burnt sausages.

Jamie: I don't but at least my hiccups have stopped!

2 Comprehension

a) Put the sentences in the correct order to summarise the dialogue.

1d) Tom, Nicola and Louise arrive at Tom's house.

a) Tom throws a tea towel over the burning sausages.

b) Jamie wants some water and smells something burning.

c) Tom's mother asks him to give his brother something to eat.

d) Tom, Nicola and Louise arrive at Tom's house.

e) They go into the sitting room to watch TV.

f) They start to grill some sausages.

g) They decide what to eat.

b) Now write the story in the past tense.

Tom, Nicola and Louise arrived at Tom's house.

3 ⌣ Useful phrases

Listen and repeat.

- No problem! • Yum! • Sounds great!
- Can I give you a hand?
- No [hot dogs] for me, thanks. • Relax!
- What's that [smell]?

4 Vocabulary

Verbs connected with food and cooking

a) Match the pictures above with these cooking terms.

- bake • boil • burn • chop • fry
- grate • grill • mash • scramble • slice

b) Write the past participle for each verb.

Infinitive   Past participle
to grill   *grilled*

5 Over to you

Talk about your favourite food and the way you like it cooked. Then say which food you don't like.

I like fried potatoes best and I quite like mashed potatoes too. I don't like grated carrot.

6 ⌣ Soundbite

Elision between two consonants

baked potatoes   fried bread
(Look at page 122.)

7 Discussion

Why are people vegetarian?
Is anyone in your class vegetarian?
What do they eat?
Do you agree with them?

Grammar flash

Verbs *should* **and** *ought to*

You **should/ought to** try these hot dogs. They're good.
You **shouldn't/ought not to** have the grill too hot.

Note

We use *should* and *ought to* when we give advice or make a strong suggestion. They mean the same, but *should* is more common.

8 Practice

Complete the advice with *should/shouldn't* **or** *ought/ought not*.

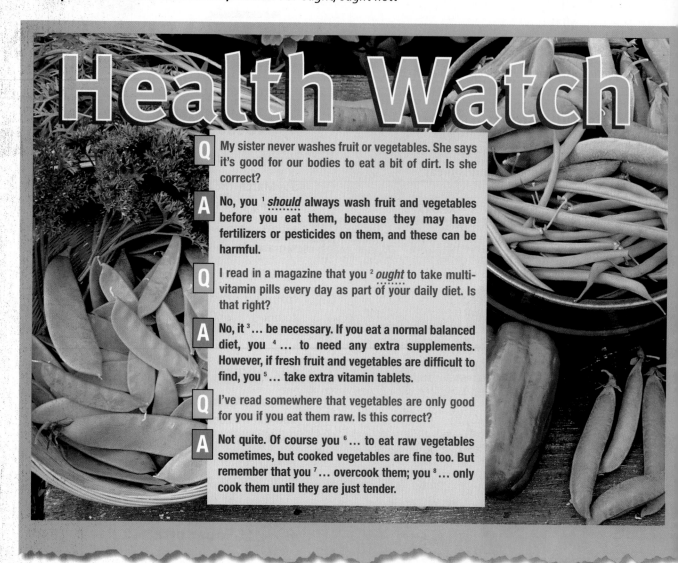

Health Watch

Q My sister never washes fruit or vegetables. She says it's good for our bodies to eat a bit of dirt. Is she correct?

A No, you ¹ *should* always wash fruit and vegetables before you eat them, because they may have fertilizers or pesticides on them, and these can be harmful.

Q I read in a magazine that you ² *ought* to take multi-vitamin pills every day as part of your daily diet. Is that right?

A No, it ³... be necessary. If you eat a normal balanced diet, you ⁴... to need any extra supplements. However, if fresh fruit and vegetables are difficult to find, you ⁵... take extra vitamin tablets.

Q I've read somewhere that vegetables are only good for you if you eat them raw. Is this correct?

A Not quite. Of course you ⁶... to eat raw vegetables sometimes, but cooked vegetables are fine too. But remember that you ⁷... overcook them; you ⁸... only cook them until they are just tender.

9 Listening helpline

Use visual context to help you listen

Always read the task and questions and look at any pictures before you listen. You can use them to predict what you are going to hear.

10 Listen

Listen to Ryan and Vicki and answer the questions.

1 What has happened?
2 When did it happen?
3 What do Ryan and Vicki try first?
4 What does Ryan decide to do?
5 Why has he wasted his time?

Grammar snapshot

Verbs *have to* **and** *must/mustn't*

Positive

Tom **has to** get back to the hotel. He starts work at six o'clock.
I **must** buy some cream to take home. It's delicious.

Make rules.

1 We normally use ... to talk about obligations which come from other people, or from routines.
2 We normally use ... to express the feelings and wishes of the speaker.

Negative

Tom **mustn't** be late for work or he'll get the sack.
Oh, good. It's Saturday! We **don't have to** go to school.

a> Make rules.
1 We normally use ... to talk about prohibition.
2 We normally use ... to express a lack of obligation or necessity.

b> What's the difference in meaning?
1 You **don't have to** speak so loudly.
2 You **mustn't** speak so loudly.

11> Practice

Complete the dialogue below with the correct form of *must* or *have to*.

Mum: It's ten o'clock, 1 '*must* go shopping. Now Lisa, don't forget to do the ironing. Ben, can you help?
Lisa: ²... I ... do it?
Mum: Yes, you do. It's your Saturday job this week. Bye!
Lisa: OK. Let's start. Is the iron hot? Ouch!
Ben: What's the matter?
Lisa: I've burnt my hand. Where's the butter?
Ben: No, you ³... use butter on a burn. You ⁴... put your hand in water.
Lisa: ⁵... the water ... be cold?
Ben: Yes, it does. It ⁶... be ice cold but it ⁷... be warm.
Lisa: ⁸... I ... leave my hand under the tap for long?
Ben: Yes, you leave it there until your hand drops off!

12> Communication

Making requests with reasons

▶ Would you mind getting your own meal? I have to go out.
▶ No, not at all. / No problem. / Oh, all right. / Sorry, I'm afraid I can't. I ...

Make similar conversations for these situations. Continue the conversations if you can.

1 You want your neighbour to move his car. You need to get your bike out.
2 You want a friend to test your vocabulary. You've got an English exam next week.
3 You want your mother to give you a lift to the bus station. You are meeting some friends in town at five o'clock.
4 You would like to buy the new All Saints CD. You want your brother/sister to lend you some money.
5 You'd like the person sitting next to you on the bus to close the window. You're cold.

Before you read

Do you often get hiccups?
Why or when do they happen?

The long hiccup

by our medical reporter,
Mary Lawson

It all started with an Indian curry, but it ended in hospital.

For many people the subject of hiccups is a joke, but for Harry Mendis, a fifteen-year-old schoolboy from Birmingham, it was something quite different.

His hiccups began one Sunday lunchtime and continued day and night for two weeks. After the first week, Harry was desperate and his parents took him to hospital, but it took another week for the doctors to cure his attack.

Harry, who is now back at school, described what happened to him.

'I began to hiccup after eating a curry from my local takeaway. I drank a glass of water but that didn't do any good. That evening I had hiccups every four seconds. We tried everything to stop them. I held my breath and drank cold drinks. My father even tried to give me a shock but that didn't work either.'

After a week of sleepless nights, he went to hospital. The doctors took an X-ray of his chest but they couldn't find anything wrong.

'They gave me some tablets and my hiccups slowed down, but it was another week before the tablets worked completely and my hiccups stopped.'

Harry was very lucky. The world record holder is the unfortunate American farmer Charles Osborne, who hiccupped constantly for sixty-eight years. He eventually stopped in 1990, but nobody knows why.

13 › Read

Read the article about Harry and choose the correct answers.

1 Harry's hiccups lasted
   a) a week.
   b) fourteen days.
   c) twenty-eight days.

2 His hiccups started after he
   a) drank a glass of water.
   b) ate an Indian meal.
   c) went to hospital.

3 His parents decided to take him to hospital when he
   a) hiccupped for four seconds.
   b) hiccupped at night.
   c) couldn't stop hiccupping.

4 His hiccups stopped after the doctors
   a) gave him some tablets.
   b) took an X-ray of his chest.
   c) gave him a shock.

5 Harry ... the world hiccupping record.
   a) has beaten
   b) is close to beating
   c) is nowhere near beating

14 › Over to you

Look at the different methods of curing hiccups. Which is best?

If you have hiccups, I think you should jump up and down ten times.

Ten ways to cure hiccups.
1 Hold your breath and count to ten.
2 Breathe in and out of a paper bag.
3 Jump up and down ten times.
4 Ask someone to pat you on the back.
5 Pull your tongue gently.
6 Sniff some pepper and make yourself sneeze.
7 Drink a glass of water quickly.
8 Ask someone to say something that will shock you.
9 Put something cold on the back of your neck.
10 Eat some burnt toast or crushed ice.

After the fire

▪▪ Read the story and put the sentences at the bottom of the page in the correct places. Then listen and see if you were right.

Steve, what on earth is that smell?

It smells as if something's burning.

_____ .

Tom! What's happened? _____ ?

Calm down, Mum. I only burnt the sausages.

Well, it smells terrible in here. _____ .

②

What happened to this tea towel? Look, it's completely burnt.

_____ .

Well, could you put it in the bin, please? It smells horrible!

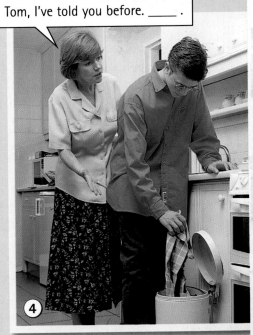

Tom, I've told you before. _____ .

④

We're really sorry, Mrs Penhale.

_____ .

How much was the tea towel? We must buy you a new one.

It's all right. _____ !

⑥

- Tom used it to put the flames out.
- You've burnt something, haven't you?
- Perhaps there's been a fire.
- You should never leave anything under a hot grill.
- You don't have to, but Tom does!
- We simply forgot about the sausages.
- I think we ought to open all the windows.

53

9 ▷ They've been bullying me.

Don't let them bully you!

Kate Martin reports

BULLYING: the facts
- 85% of children in the UK have been victims of bullying at least once.
- Bullies are more likely to commit crimes when they are older.

Charlotte's story

Last year we moved to a new town and I started at a new school. At first I was really happy about the school and I made friends with the popular girls in my year. But soon they started to pick on me because I was too 'posh'.
I think they were jealous of me because I had nice clothes. Whenever I walked past them, they called me names or tripped me up and they sometimes hit me. They even wrote nasty things about me on the desk tops. Nobody did anything about it. It was horrible. They made my life miserable. In the end I felt really sad and lonely.

Charlotte, 14, Bristol.

How can you recognise a bully?
He or she will:
- try to find your weak point – perhaps you are shy, nervous or easily upset.
- make fun of you in front of your friends.
- dare you to do something wrong, like steal something or miss school.
- borrow money then won't pay you back.
- say nasty things about you for no reason.

Posed by models

Before you read

What is a bully?
Does bullying only happen at school?

1> Read

a> Read the article and guess the meaning of these words and phrases. Check your answers with your teacher or dictionary.

- victim • at least • likely
- commit a crime • pick on
- posh • call somebody names
- trip up • nasty • miserable
- weak point • make fun of
- dare somebody to do something
- pay back • for no reason

b> Answer the questions.

1 When did Charlotte become a victim of bullying?
2 Why did the girls bully her?
3 What sort of things did they do?
4 Did anyone help Charlotte?
5 How did Charlotte feel?

2> Vocabulary helpline

Increase your word power

When you look up a new adjective and record it in your vocabulary book, it is a good idea to check if it has a noun form, and record that as well, e.g. *jealous (adj.), jealousy (n.)*. This will help you to be more flexible and creative in your speaking and writing.

3> Vocabulary

Nouns and adjectives of emotion
- happiness • misery • jealousy
- nervousness • shyness
- loneliness • nastiness

Look at the text about bullying and find the adjectives related to the nouns above.

4> Practice

Write a sentence using an appropriate adjective from Exercise 3 for each situation.

1 A: Sarah looks ...! B: Yes, she's just won some money!
2 He's very ... . He hates meeting new people.
3 She saw John with another girl last night so she is feeling ... .
4 I'm sure he's very ... . He hasn't got any friends.
5 I've got my driving test tomorrow so I'm a bit ... .
6 My sister is ... because she has to repeat a year at school.
7 Dick had a ... accident and had to go to hospital.

5> 👓 Listen

Listen to a boy talking about bullying and answer the questions.

1 When and why did the bullying start?
2 Who were the 'bullies'?
3 How did he feel about it?
4 What did the bullies do?
5 How did the bullying stop?
6 What helped him in the end?

6> Discussion

a> Look at two reasons why bullies pick on other people.

- They're from a different race or background.
- They don't have any brothers, sisters or friends to defend them.

What other reasons are there?

b> List some advice to give to people who have a problem with bullies at school.

1 It's a good idea to walk to school in a group.

c> Suggest some more general ways to tackle the problem of bullying.

7 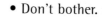 Listen and read

Tom: Jamie, can you take this video back to the rental shop for me, please?

Jamie: Sorry, I'm reading my book.

Tom: You've been reading that book for days!

Jamie: So? Anyway, I'm going to have a shower in a moment.

Tom: Oh, come on, Jamie! Do me a favour for once! It's not far to the shop.

Jamie: No.

Tom: Why not?

Jamie: Well, if you must know, I don't want to go past Rick Ward's house.

Tom: Rick Ward! That creep! Why?

Jamie: Because he and his friends always pick on me when I go past.

Tom: What do you mean 'pick on' you?

Jamie: They call me names and push me around.

Tom: How long has this been going on?

Jamie: Since the beginning of term.

Tom: Would you like me to go and sort them out?

Jamie: No, it's OK. Give me the video. Shall I get another one for you?

Tom: No, don't bother. Jamie, are you sure you'll be all right?

Jamie: I'll be fine!

8 Comprehension

Complete the information.

Jamie's excuses for not taking back the video:
Jamie's real reason:
Examples of the bullies' behaviour:
When the bullying started:
Tom's offer:
Jamie's decision:

9 Useful phrases

Listen and repeat.

- Do me a favour [for once]!
- Why not?
- If you must know, [...].
- What do you mean?
- Don't bother.

10> Communication

Offering, accepting or refusing help

▶ Would you like me to talk to him?
▶ Yes, please. That's very kind of you.

▶ Shall I do the shopping for you?
▶ No, don't worry. I can do it myself./I can manage, thanks.

In pairs, offer and accept or refuse help in the following situations.

A friend has invited you over to lunch and to watch a video.

1 When you arrive you notice that your friend is laying the table.
2 You finish your meal and there is a lot of washing-up.
3 Your friend has to take the video back to the shop. You pass the video shop on your way home.

11> Write

Write a letter to an English-speaking friend who lives near you.

• You have just read in a magazine that your favourite band are giving a concert soon in your town. (Say when and where.)

• Offer to find out details about the concert and get two tickets.

Dear Jerry,
I have just found out that ... are
giving a concert at ... on ... .

COMING SOUTH SOON
LUCKY NORTH
THE BAND YOU'VE ALL BEEN WAITING FOR!
SATURDAY 19TH SEPTEMBER 7.30 PM
SPORTS CENTRE
TICKETS £15.50 AND £13.50
TICKETLINE: 01637 3332220

Grammar snapshot

Present perfect continuous with *for* and *since*

Positive statements	Negative statements
I've been reading **for** an hour.	I haven't been reading **for** very long.
He's been waiting **since** 8 o'clock.	He hasn't been waiting **for** very long.

Questions	Short answers
Have you been reading this book?	Yes, I have. / No, I haven't.
Has she been watching a video?	Yes, she has. / No, she hasn't.

Note
One use of the present perfect continuous is to talk about events and actions which begin in the past and continue up to the present moment. It can be used in answer to the question *How long?*
How long has this been going on?
It's been **going on** for a long time/since the beginning of term.

12> ⊙ Soundbite

Weak form / bɪn /
Have you **been** waiting long?   (Look at page 122.)

13> Practice

Make questions and answers with *How long?* and the present perfect continuous.

A: *How long have you been trying to phone me?*
B: *I've been trying to phone you for half an hour.*

1 you/try/to phone me? (half an hour)
2 the chicken/cook/in the oven? (about twenty minutes)
3 Carl Schmidt/play football/for Brazil? (start of the season)
4 he/clean his motorbike? (two hours)
5 you/wait to see the doctor? (nine o'clock)
6 your sister/live in Florida? (over a year)

14> Over to you

Talk about one or more of the following topics by using the cues.

Do any extra activities after school? (How long/do it/them?)
Got a boy/girlfriend (How long/go out with him/her?)
What sport/play well? (How long/play it?)
Play an instrument? (How long/learn it?)

A: *Do you do any extra activities after school?*
B: *Yes, I do. I sing in a band.*
A: *How long have you been doing that?*
B: *For a year.*

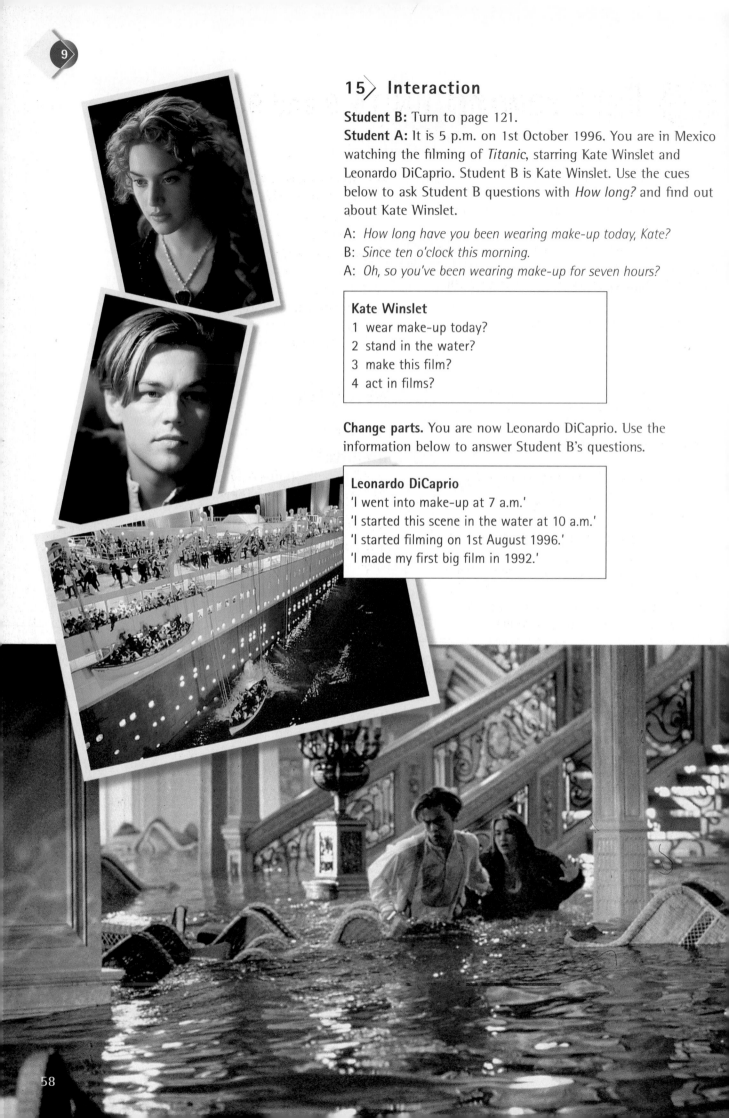

15 Interaction

Student B: Turn to page 121.

Student A: It is 5 p.m. on 1st October 1996. You are in Mexico watching the filming of *Titanic*, starring Kate Winslet and Leonardo DiCaprio. Student B is Kate Winslet. Use the cues below to ask Student B questions with *How long?* and find out about Kate Winslet.

A: *How long have you been wearing make-up today, Kate?*

B: *Since ten o'clock this morning.*

A: *Oh, so you've been wearing make-up for seven hours?*

Kate Winslet
1 wear make-up today?
2 stand in the water?
3 make this film?
4 act in films?

Change parts. You are now Leonardo DiCaprio. Use the information below to answer Student B's questions.

Leonardo DiCaprio
'I went into make-up at 7 a.m.'
'I started this scene in the water at 10 a.m.'
'I started filming on 1st August 1996.'
'I made my first big film in 1992.'

Fast rewind UNITS 8 and 9

Grammar

1 Give advice for the situations using *shouldn't* and *ought to*.

I never seem to wake up in time for school. (stay up so late/go to bed earlier)
You shouldn't stay up so late. You ought to go to bed earlier.

1 I don't have any friends. (be so serious all the time/join a club or something)
2 I can't afford to go to the cinema so often. (spend so much on CDs/save some money)
3 I like lots of different sports but I'm not brilliant at any of them. (try to do so much/focus on one sport)
4 My hair is impossible! (wash it so often/leave it for a few days between washes)

2 Choose the correct verb in each sentence.

It's great to see you. You *must*/*ought to* come in and have a cup of tea!

1 We love Sundays because we *ought not to*/*don't have to* get up early.
2 Of course you're hot. You *shouldn't*/*mustn't* have the heating on!
3 The trouble with not living near school is that I *must*/*have to* get up so early in the morning.
4 You look tired. You *ought to*/*have to* take a holiday.
5 Nicola is pleased that she *mustn't*/*doesn't have to* do the early morning shift very often.
6 You *mustn't*/*don't have to* leave without seeing the Picasso exhibition.

3 Complete the sentences with the correct form of *have to*.

I'm afraid I can't come out tonight. I ... my project. (finish)
I'm afraid I can't come out tonight. I have to finish my project.

1 My sister ... for a visa to go to the USA. (apply)
2 I'm really glad that I ... Latin at school. (not/learn)
3 ... military service? (your brother/do)
4 Students ... high grades to enter medical school. (get)
5 I'm sorry you failed the exam. ... it again? (you/take)
6 My mother ... to work on Saturdays any more. (not/go)
7 ... extra for taking the bike on the train? (you/pay)
8 Nicola is pleased that she ... do the early morning shift very often. (not/do)
9 We love Sundays because we ... early (not/get up)

4 Make sentences using the present perfect continuous tense with *since* or *for*.

Nicola/work/in the hotel/a week.
Nicola has been working in the hotel for a week.

1 Do you realise, I/wait here/two o'clock!
2 She/live in Spain/six months.
3 He/wear/contact lenses/at least five years.
4 My father/work for the same company/1994.
5 They/run/the lottery in the UK/many years.
6 I/collect/stamps/I was seven.

Vocabulary

5 Match each verb with a suitable food or drink.

1d) grilled fish

1 grilled 2 grated 3 iced 4 mashed 5 sliced 6 boiled
a) eggs b) potatoes c) cheese d) fish e) water f) onion

6 Complete the endings of the nouns.

nasty nast*iness*

1 shy shy... 2 lonely lonel... 3 jealous jealous...
4 happy happ... 5 miserable miser...

Communication

7 Reorder the sentences to complete the conversation.

A: *I'm going into town now, Mrs Simpson.*

a) Yes, please. Here's a £5 note.
b) Not at all. Do you want it to go first class?
c) No problem. Would you like me to get anything else?
d) Oh, are you? Would you mind posting a parcel for me?
e) No, that's fine. See you later. Bye!
f) No, don't bother. But could you get me some milk on your way home?
g) Fine. Shall I get a receipt for you?

Progress update Units 8 and 9

How do you rate your progress? Tick the chart.

	Excellent ★★★★	Good ★★★	OK ★★	Can do better ★
Grammar				
Vocabulary				
Communication				

Stowaway

A seventeen-year-old deaf-and-dumb schoolboy has become a household name in his home country of Russia. Roman Venkov, who can only communicate by sign language or by writing, claims that for two years he travelled to seventeen countries without a passport or money.

One night two years ago, Roman quietly left his home in St Petersburg. He didn't tell his mother that he was going, and he had no money. He wanted to see the world. First he travelled south across Russia to the Black Sea and stowed away on a boat to Turkey. Then he travelled to Greece and from there through Europe to the Belgian coast, from where he stowed away on a ferry across the Channel to Dover in England.

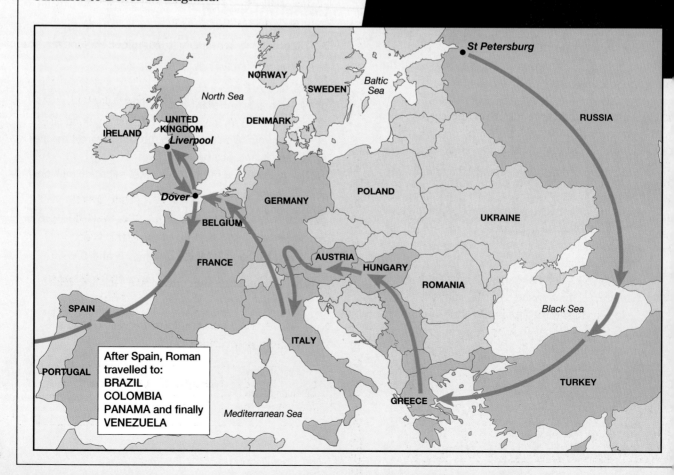

After Spain, Roman travelled to:
BRAZIL
COLOMBIA
PANAMA and finally
VENEZUELA

hen the British police arrested him, oman told them in sign language that his ame was Michael and that he was English. 'hey sent me to a family in Liverpool,' says oman. 'The mother could speak sign anguage because her parents were both eaf and dumb. She looked after me and was very happy.'

However, at the age of sixteen, the ritish social services sent him to a special chool for orphans. He hated this school and itchhiked back to Dover. Here he secretly ot on a train which took him through the hannel Tunnel to France. In France he egged for money on the streets to survive. a Spain he persuaded the Brazilian consul hat he was Brazilian and was called José io Branco! The consul gave Roman a assport and paid his air fare to Rio de aneiro. 'But Brazil did not feel like home so moved on.' This time he went by boat to 'olombia, then to Panama and, finally, to is seventeenth country, Venezuela.

By now Roman was feeling homesick. ome Russian people told their consul about im. The consul discovered that he came rom St Petersburg and agreed to pay for his ight to Moscow. Two years after leaving St 'etersburg, Roman was safely home. Since is return, he has appeared on TV and given ewspaper interviews about his remarkable ourney.

The Russian authorities have been iscussing whether they should punish him ut they probably won't. 'He hasn't actually een on a luxury cruise, has he? In fact his ife has been quite hard,' said one official. oman says, 'I know I've done wrong and 'm not going to run away again. I have to ettle down now and do some school work. But at least I've seen what life is like broad. There are no great surprises.'

1〉 Read

a〉 Read the article and trace Roman's journey on the map.

b〉 Answer the questions.

1 Why was Roman's journey extraordinary?
2 Why did he like Liverpool?
3 Why did he run away from Liverpool?
4 How did he live in France?
5 How did he get to Brazil?
6 Why didn't he stay there?
7 How did he get home to Russia?
8 What has been doing since he returned home?
9 What have the Russian authorities decided to do about him?
10 What has he discovered about life?

2〉 Discussion

Do you think that Roman's journey was wrong?
How did he deceive so many people?
How did people feel when they discovered the truth about Roman?
What does Roman's story tell you about people?

3〉 Write

Imagine Roman has just arrived back home in Russia. Write a short interview with him in the form of a dialogue.

You: *You've just returned from Venezuela, haven't you?*

Roman: *That's right.*

You: *Tell me about your trip. When did you leave Russia?*

4〉 ⟨••⟩ Listen

a〉 Listen to Rachel talking about her travels. She started in Hong Kong. Copy the chart and put these places in the first column in the order in which she mentions them.

• Brussels • China • Laos • London • Malaysia
• Russia • Singapore • Thailand • Vietnam

b〉 Listen again and complete the rest of the information in the chart.

To	By	Length of stay	Activities
Singapore	*air*	*1 week*	

Project ▶ ② Snapshot of a television programme

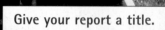

A ▶ A TV news report

Write a report for an English-language television news programme. Choose a story which is in the news in your country and collect information and pictures about it to illustrate your report.

Give your report a title.

Puma or ordinary cat? The mystery continues .

Summarise the news story.

The so-called 'Beast of Bodmin Moor' has appeared once again. It turned up again last week in a Cornish field. The 'beast' is a large, cat-like creature almost as big as a puma, which many people think has been running wild on Bodmin Moor for

Describe what happened in more detail.

The animal appeared yesterday while a local man was walking his dog. It

Give your story a conclusion.

At a press conference yesterday, the man showed a video of 'the beast'. He

B ▶ TV soap opera or drama

Invent a TV soap opera or drama. Give it a title and write a brief description of it. You can use these character types to help you.

- Mr Nice Guy
- Miss Nice Girl
- Mr Bad Guy
- Miss Bad Girl
- the good friends
- the mixed-up kid
- the mysterious stranger
- the gossip

Where is it set and who are the main characters?

'Eastenders' is set in a square in the east end of London. The main characters are members of families who live and work in the area. Two central characters are the Mitchell brothers; Grant, the bad guy, and Phil who is a good guy but is very mixed-up. Grant is married to Tiffany and they have a baby daughter called

What is happening in some of the current storylines?

Grant and Tiffany aren't getting on very well and she has decided to

What happened in the last episode?

In the last episode, when Grant arrived home,

2 Take a break

I just called to say "I love you"

Stevie Wonder was born in Detroit, Michigan in 1950. In spite of being blind since birth, he played the organ, harmonica, bongos and drums when he was a boy. The producers at Motown Records in Detroit soon recognised his talents and gave him a recording contract as 'Little Stevie Wonder'. He grew up to be one of the great recording artists of the century. His song *I just called to say 'I love you'* was used in the film *Woman in Red* in 1984 and was his first British number one hit single. It has become one of the most well-known romantic ballads in the world.

1⟩ 👀 **Listen to the song and note the following things in the order you hear them. Then look at the back of the book to check your answers.**

a) southern skies   b) autumn breeze   c) tender August night
d) first of spring   e) Halloween   f) warm July   g) flowers
h) Christmas joy   i) New Year's Day   j) April rain   k) my heart
l) wedding   m) Libra sun

2⟩ Look at the chart below. Listen to the song again and list the words which fit the categories. Look at the back of the book to check your answers.

Days and special events	Months of the year	Seasons of the year
1 *New Year's Day*	1	1
2	2	2
3	3	3
4	4	

3⟩ Guess the meaning of these phrases from the song.

- chocolate covered candy hearts   • no flowers bloom
- the bottom of my heart   • a harvest moon   • falling leaves
- birds (which) fly to southern skies

4⟩ What gifts would you send a boy/girlfriend? Which is the most popular gift in the class?

Unless I get to bed, ...

Learning goals

Communication
Talk about future possibility
Show surprise

Grammar
Verbs *will/won't*, *may* or *might*
for predictions
First conditional: *if/unless* clause
+ *'ll (will)/won't*
Negative questions

Vocabulary
Verb *get*
Parts of the body

1 > •• Listen and read

Jake: Hi, Nicola!

Nicola: Oh, hello Jake. Aren't you surfing today?

Jake: No, I'm having a break. How's it going?

Tom: We're busy.

Nicola: I'm trying to teach Tom to bowl. I won't be long. Come on, Tom. You might get a strike.

Jake: I just wanted to ask you something. There's a sixties disco at the surf club tonight. I was wondering – would you like to go?

Nicola: Yes, I'd love to. The only trouble is, I'm doing the early morning shift tomorrow.

Jake: So?

Nicola: Unless I get to bed before midnight, I won't get up in time for work.

Jake: Why don't you swap shifts with someone?

Nicola: Good idea! I may be able to swap with Tom. I'll ask him.

Nicola: Tom, can you do me a favour?

Tom: It depends what it is.

Nicola: I'd like to go to a disco with Jake tonight. Could you do my early morning shift tomorrow?

Tom: Oh, all right. If you do one of mine.

Nicola: OK. If you do mine tomorrow, I'll do yours on Friday.

Tom: It's a deal.

2 > Comprehension

Answer T (true), F (false) or DK (don't know).

1 Jake has come to see Tom.
2 Jake invites Nicola out for the evening.
3 The disco has a special theme.
4 Nicola is often late for work in the morning.
5 Nicola wants to change her working hours.
6 Tom refuses to change shifts.

Grammar snapshot

Verbs *will/won't, may* or *might* **for predictions**

Positive statements
Jake **will** be at the disco. (It's definite.)
Louise **may/might** come. (It's possible.)

Negative statements
Tom **won't** be there. (It's definite.)
Louise **may not/might not** come. (It's possible.)

Questions	Short answers
Will Jake be at the disco?	Yes, he **will**.
Will Tom be there?	No, he **won't**.
Will Louise be there?	She **may/might**.

What's the difference in meaning?
1 I think Nicola **will go** to the disco with Jake.
2 I think Nicola **may/might go** to the disco with Jake.

3 ⬝⬝ Useful phrases

Listen and repeat.

- I was wondering ...
- The only trouble is, ...
- Can you do me a favour?
- It depends ...
- All right.
- It's a deal.

4 ⬝⬝ Sound**bite**

The sound / l / in initial, medial and final position

Let's   Nicola   I'll   (Look at page 123.)

5 Practice

Talk about what you think will happen at the Surf Club disco.

1 What music will they play? (Give the names of any groups or singers from the 1960s you know.)
2 What clothes will they wear? (What colours? What patterns? What styles?)
3 What will they eat and drink?
4 When will it end?

A: *I think they'll play ...*
B: *Yes, and they may/might ...*
A: *They definitely won't ...*
   and they'll probably ...

Newquay Surf Club

1960s DISCO
HARD DAY'S NIGHT
WEDNESDAY 5TH AUGUST
8 TILL LATE
NEWQUAY TOWN HALL
PRIZES FOR TEN BEST 1960s OUTFITS

6 Write

Write a paragraph about what you think will happen at the Surf Club disco.

Tall stories

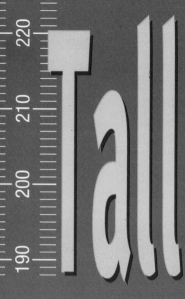

This week *Good Health* investigates the facts and exposes some of the myths about height and growth. Are the statements true or false?

1 We are a lot taller than our grandparents' generation.

True Each generation is an average 2.5 cm taller than the previous generation. They say that by the year 2100 people will be 15 cm taller than they are now.

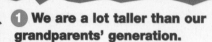

2 You will grow faster if your parents cuddle and kiss you.

Children who do not get affection switch off their growth hormone. It seems when you are stressed, you produce chemicals which may interfere with the growth hormone.

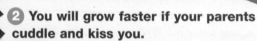

3 If you smoke, you won't reach your maximum potential height.

There is no real evidence of this. However, if a pregnant woman smokes, her baby may be smaller at birth than the baby of a similar non-smoking woman. Also, at the age of seven, children of smokers are usually shorter than children of non-smokers.

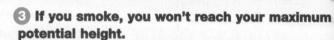

4 You won't grow to your maximum height unless you get enough sleep.

More growth hormone is released when you are asleep at night than during the day.

5 Eating green vegetables helps you to grow.

If you eat a healthy diet, which includes green vegetables, you will grow to your full maximum height.

6 If you live in the country, you will grow taller than if you live in the city.

Many people think that children who live in the country are healthier, but in fact children who live in cities are on average taller than country children.

7 Mothers are usually shorter than their sons.

A son will always be taller than his mother unless his father is at least 12 cm shorter than his mother.

8 You don't grow after the age of 19.

Most people stop growing between the ages of 16 and 18 but if you are a late-developer, you may continue to grow until you are 21 or 22. In their teenage years, young people usually grow 20% of their final height.

7〉 Read

a〉 Look at the text opposite. Read the paragraph headings and say which statements are true and which are false.

b〉 Read the complete text and check your answers.

c〉 Guess the meaning of these words and phrases.

- tall story   • investigate   • expose   • myth
- generation   • previous   • cuddle   • switch off
- hormone   • chemical   • interfere with   • potential
- pregnant   • release   • late-developer

8〉 Comprehension

Answer T (true) or F (false).

1 In the year 2100 girls will be taller than they are now.
2 If children feel stressed and unloved, they don't grow as fast as children who are loved.
3 Smoking stops people from growing.
4 Boys and girls who live in the country are on average taller than those who live in a town.
5 If a tall woman has a much shorter husband, her sons may be shorter than her.
6 The growth hormone is most active after the age of 16.

Grammar snapshot

First conditional: *if/unless* **clause +** *'ll (will)/won't*

a) What are the missing words?
1 **If** you do mine tomorrow, I ... do yours on Friday.
2 **If** I don't go to bed before midnight, I ... get up in time for work.
3 **Unless** I go to bed before midnight, I ... get up in time for work.

b) Make a rule by choosing *present* **or** *future*.
The verb in the *if* or *unless* clause is in the present/future tense, and the verb in the main clause is in the present/future tense.

Notes
- *will* and *won't* can be replaced by *may* or *might*.
  If I don't go to bed before midnight, I **may not/might not** wake up in time for work.
- *unless* means *if ... not*

9〉 Practice

In pairs, match the clauses to make complete sentences, using *will/won't* **or** *may/might*.

1 b) If you eat a lot, you won't necessarily put on weight.

1 If you (eat) a lot,
2 If your parents (be) tall and thin,
3 If you (not use up) much energy,
4 If you (not need) all the food you eat,
5 If you (diet) a lot,

a) you (probably/be) tall and thin too.
b) you (not necessarily put on) weight.
c) you (not look/your best).
d) you (not need) to eat so much.
e) your body (store) the food as fat.

10〉 Over to you

Talk about these questions.

What sort of advice about your health do your parents give you?
Is it always sensible?
Do you always take the advice?

11〉 Memory bank

Parts of the body

Write down as many words as you can for parts of the body

a) above the waist.
b) below the waist.

12〉 〔••〕 Listen

Listen to a young girl talking about her training as a gymnast and answer the questions.

1 How old was she when she started?
2 How often did she train?
3 What problems are there if young gymnasts train too hard?
4 What were her injuries?
5 How did they affect her training?
6 What has been a worse injury? Why?

13 〉 Communication

Showing surprise

▶ Aren't you surfing today?
▶ No, I'm having a break.

▶ Haven't you finished yet?
▶ No, it's more difficult than I thought.

Look at the pictures below. In pairs, use negative questions to show surprise. Then continue each conversation if you can.

1. Your friend hasn't finished last week's homework.

2. Your friend doesn't like chocolate ice cream.

3. Your friend didn't watch the football match on television last night.

4. Your friend can't swim.

5. Your friend isn't going to come back to school next year.

14 〉 Vocabulary helpline

Record meanings in sentences

When you look up a verb like *get* in a big dictionary, you will see that it has several meanings. Next to each meaning is an example sentence. Copy the sentences you think will be useful into your vocabulary notebook.

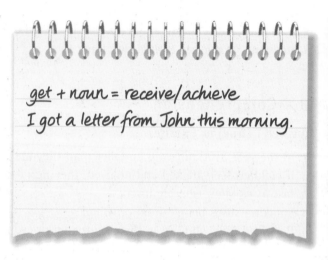

get + noun = receive/achieve
I got a letter from John this morning.

15 〉 Vocabulary

Verb *get*

Get with different parts of speech	Meanings
a) *get* + noun	receive/achieve buy/fetch
b) *get* + adjective	become
c) *get* + past participle	achieve a different state
d) *get to* + noun	reach/arrive at

a〉 Match the meanings of the verb *get* **with these sentences.**

1. The food is **getting** cold.
2. I **got** a letter from John this morning.
3. She **got** to Newquay at 5 p.m.
4. They **got** married in Las Vegas.
5. Can you **get** me some milk?

b〉 Match the words and phrases below with meanings a) – d) above. Then write a sentence for each.

school – d)   I get to school at 8.00 every day.

• school   • a newspaper   • angry   • changed
• better   • engaged   • dressed   • work
• good marks   • a phone call   • bed   • Paris

Trouble for Jamie

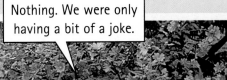

Read the story and put the pictures in the correct order. Then listen and see if you were right.

1 = Picture F

OK. You go first, I'll follow you. If they do anything to you, they'll get a surprise from me.

Hold it! What do you think you're doing to my brother?

Nothing. We were only having a bit of a joke.

Well, it's not funny! Now, clear off!

B

Can't you just leave me alone!

We'll go away if you give us that five pound note.

Come on. Give us your money!

C

Tom, can you do me a favour?

It depends what it is.

Could you come with me to the corner shop? Rick and Mark might be there.

D

We'll get you one day, Jamie Penhale. Just you wait!

Jamie, could you get me some milk from the corner shop, please? Here's five pounds.

But the shop might be shut. It's one o'clock.

Don't be silly, Jamie. You know it won't be shut.

F

Well, look who it isn't. Baby Jamie!

Going shopping for mummy, are you?

G

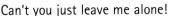

Learning goals

Communication
Describe processes
Complain, request and apologise

Grammar
The passive: present and past simple

Vocabulary
Adjectives to describe behaviour

1 ▷ 👁 Listen and read

Woman: Excuse me. I've been waiting for half an hour. Can I order now, please?

Nicola: Yes, of course. I'll get you a menu. Sorry to keep you waiting.

Woman: Are the eggs free-range?

Nicola: Yes, they are. They were delivered fresh from the farm today.

Man: Excuse me. I've got an early train to catch tomorrow morning. Could I have breakfast at six o'clock, please?

Nicola: I'm afraid that isn't possible, sir. Breakfast isn't served until seven.

Man: But I only want coffee, toast and marmalade. Surely that's possible?

Nicola: I'm afraid there's nothing I can do about it, sir.

Man: Oh, forget it!

Nicola: Well, it's not my fault!

Morris: Nicola, you're expected to be polite and helpful to our guests at all times. Is that clear?

Nicola: Yes. Sorry, Morris.

70

2 Comprehension

Answer the questions.

1 Why is the woman unhappy?
2 What does she want to know?
3 Why does the man want an early breakfast?
4 What explanation does Nicola give to him?
5 What does Morris think of Nicola's behaviour?

3 Useful phrases

Listen and repeat.

- Sorry to [keep you waiting].
- There's nothing I can do about it.
- Oh, forget it!
- It's not my fault!
- Is that clear?

4 Vocabulary

Adjectives to describe behaviour

- (un)kind   • (im)polite   • rude
- (un)friendly   • (un)helpful
- (un)critical   • stupid   • sensible

Answer the questions below. (There may be more than one answer.)

What do you call someone who:

1 always says 'Please' and 'Thank you'? *polite*
2 never says 'Hello' when you meet?
3 never offers help?
4 always does the right thing?
5 always complains about things?
6 says or does silly things?
7 often says cruel things?
8 never says 'Thank you'?

5 Communication

Complaining, requesting and apologising

▶ Excuse me. I've been waiting for a quarter of an hour. Can I order now?
▶ Yes, of course. Sorry to keep you waiting.

▶ I'm afraid I can't sleep. The noise from the disco is terrible. Could you do something about it?
▶ Sorry about that. I'll ask the DJ to turn it down.

▶ I'm afraid our television doesn't work. Could somebody come and repair it?
▶ I'm sorry about that. I'll send somebody to have a look at it. Will tomorrow be all right?

In pairs, use the pictures to make similar polite conversations.

1 A: *Excuse me. I'm afraid this sweater has shrunk. It was the first time I washed it and I didn't use hot water. Can you do something about it?*
  B: ...

A: sweater/shrink/ do something?
B: refund the money

A: car/break down again/ repair it?
B: send someone to look at it

A: toast/burn/ bring some more?
B: get you some immediately

A: you/make a lot of noise/ be quiet?
B: go somewhere else

71

Grammar snapshot

The passive: present and past simple

a) Look at the sentences below. Which are active and which are passive?

Present

1 Breakfast **is served** from 7 a.m.
2 We **serve** breakfast from 7 a.m.

Past

3 The eggs **were delivered** this morning.
4 They **delivered** the eggs this morning.

b) Make rules by choosing the correct alternative. We use the passive:

1 when we are *interested in/not interested in* who or what causes something to happen.
2 for *formal/informal* notices and announcements.

6 ⟩ Practice

You are visiting a farm. Rewrite the questions more formally in the passive.

How often do they collect the eggs?
How often are the eggs collected?

What time did they collect them yesterday?
What time were they collected yesterday?

1 Where do you keep the hens?
2 How many eggs did you produce last year?
3 How often do they milk the cows?
4 Do they make any cheese on the farm?
5 Why did you sell the horses?
6 Did you grow any potatoes last year?
7 Do you sell fruit locally, or do you export it?
8 When did they build the new barn?
9 What do they use it for?

7 ⟩ Interaction

Student B: Turn to page 121.
Student A: Ask Student B questions to complete the chart at the bottom of the page about different crops and their food products. Try to add some information of your own about each crop.

A: *Where are olives grown?*
B: *Olives are grown in countries like Spain, Italy, Greece and Turkey.*
A: *What are they used for?*
B: *They're used to make olive oil, which is exported all over the world. They're also used as a basic food.*

8 ⟩ Over to you

Talk to your partner about products from your country using these verbs.

• produce • grow • make • export

A: *I think apples are grown in … .*

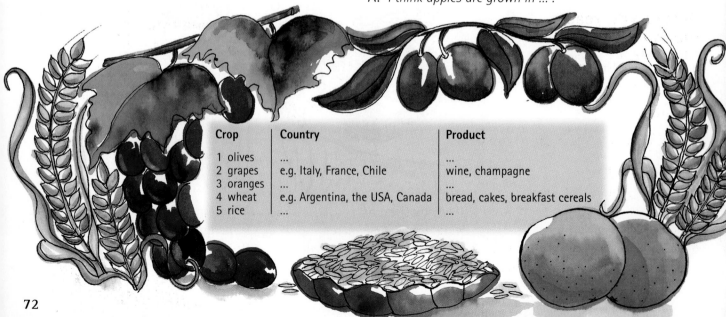

Crop	Country	Product
1 olives	...	...
2 grapes	e.g. Italy, France, Chile	wine, champagne
3 oranges	...	...
4 wheat	e.g. Argentina, the USA, Canada	bread, cakes, breakfast cereals
5 rice	...	...

Farming today
– the dream and the reality

by **Alan Marsh**

For many people, the idea of a perfect farm is the one you often see on television commercials. These show fields of corn, one or two cows and sheep happily grazing, and chickens scratching in the farmyard. The reality of modern farming is very different in many countries.

Small farms do still exist, but the demand for cheap food has forced many farmers in Britain to use intensive methods of farming. Animals like calves, pigs and chickens are treated as if they were on a production line in a factory, and so the term 'factory farming' is now widely used.

One example of factory farming is the 'battery hen' system. In the past, hens were kept in the open farmyard during the day. They were allowed to walk around freely and were given space to scratch and to stretch their wings. At night they were put in hen houses.

Today, most hens in Britain are locked up for twenty-four hours a day in wire cages or 'batteries', 50 cm by 50 cm, with sloping floors. Five hens are put in one cage and up to six cages are stacked on top of each other. Thousands of hens are kept like this in one building. There are over thirty-three million battery hens in Britain.

Of course, battery cages are very clean and hygienic. The hens are warm and safe from predators like foxes, but they are kept in a very small space. They can't flap their wings or clean their feathers properly. The wire floors are sharp, so the hens' feet are often damaged and their claws are broken. There is nowhere quiet for them to lay their eggs. There is no straw for them to scratch or peck, so they peck at other hens instead and sometimes all their feathers drop out.

Most people prefer the idea – and the taste – of free-range meat from animals which are allowed to move around outside. They also prefer organic products which are grown without pesticides or fertilizers. The trouble is that food produced in these ways is expensive. If people want cheap food, factory farming will probably continue.

Before you read
What does 'factory farming' mean?
Which animals are 'factory farmed'?

9 > Read

a > **Read the article and check your answers.**

b > **Guess the meaning of these words.**

- corn • graze (v.) • scratch (v.) • demand
- intensive • treat (v.) • production line
- battery • wire • cage • sloping • stack (v.)
- predator • damage (v.) • straw • drop out (v.)
- free-range • organic • pesticide • fertilizer

c > **Answer the questions about hens.**

1 Where were hens kept in the past?
2 Where are they kept now?
3 What were the advantages of the old system?
4 What are the advantages of the present system?

10 > •• Soundbite

Syllable deletion

interested   difference   (Look at page 123.)

11 ⟩ 🔊 Listen

Listen to a farmer talking about modern farming methods and answer the questions.

1 What sort of farm does he own?
2 For how many generations have the members of his family been farmers?
3 In what ways has farming changed?
4 What does he think of:
   a) veal calves?   b) organic farming?

12 ⟩ Discussion

What do you think of factory farming?
Does it exist in your country?
Are there any other problems with farming methods in your country?

13 ⟩ Writing helpline

Formal letters

Match each of these instructions with the correct number on the letter.

a) 4

a) Begin a formal letter *Dear Mr/Mrs/ Miss/Ms ...* or *Dear Sir/Madam.*

b) Close with *Yours sincerely* if you have begun with *Dear Mr/ Mrs,* etc. or close with *Yours faithfully* if you have begun with *Dear Sir/Madam.*

c) In your first sentence say why you are writing.

d) On the left-hand side write the full name and address of the recipient.

e) Sign your name and then write it clearly underneath in capital letters, with your title (*Mr/ Mrs,* etc.).

f) Write the date below your address.

g) Write your address (but not your name) in the top right-hand corner.

14 ⟩ Write

Write a letter to a newspaper using these notes to protest about how veal calves are treated. Try to include verbs in the passive.

- take the calves from their mothers when two weeks old
- put them in veal crates: small dark cages with a concrete floor and no straw
- calves cannot turn round or lie down comfortably
- feed them on a liquid milk diet, low in iron and fibre
- kill them when six months old

① 28 Harbour Road,
St Ives,
Cornwall
TR26 2AJ

② The Editor
Newquay Times,
Ship Street,
Newquay,
Cornwall
TR7 2PQ

③ 30th June

④ Dear Sir,

⑤ I am writing to protest about the way veal calves are treated in many parts of Europe.

....

I think you should tell your readers not to order veal in restaurants. This may help to stop such a cruel way of producing food.

⑥ Yours faithfully,

⑦ *Gavin Merton*
(MR GAVIN MERTON)

Fast rewind UNITS 11 and 12

Grammar

1 Complete the conversation with *will, won't* or *might*.

A: Do you think England [1] *will* win the World Cup?
B: No, I don't think they [2] ... . What do you think, Ben?
A: No, England definitely [3] ... win but I think Spain [4] ... .
B: Really? Do you think they have a chance?
A: Yes, I do. We [5] ... have to wait and see, [6] ... we!

2 Complete the sentences with *if* or *unless*.

I'm sure they'll come *if* you ask them.

1 ... you've got too many copies, I'll take one.
2 Your English won't improve ... you speak more in class.
3 I'll lend you some money ... you need it.
4 I'll phone you ... I can't come this evening.
5 Don't worry! ... I'm very ill, I'm coming on holiday!
6 Don't look at the TV screen now ... you want to know the result.
7 ... you shout at her, she'll burst into tears.

3 Complete the sentences with the correct form of the verbs in brackets.

If it costs a lot, I ... it. (not/buy)
If it costs a lot, I won't buy it.

1 Careful! It ... if you drop it. (break)
2 If you ... me nicely, I'll tell you a secret. (ask)
3 Unless he's very late, I ... anything. (not/say)
4 What will we do if there ... a train to London? (not/be)
5 If he ... any problems, he'll phone you. (have)
6 We'll come at seven if we ... from you. (not/hear)
7 If you win some money, ... me out for the evening? (you/take)
8 You ... a pay rise unless you ask. (not/get)

4 Complete the text with the verbs in the correct form of the present or past passive.

Farm diary

Last year was an unusual year on the farm. Normally the crops (harvest) [1] *are harvested* in July and the fruit (pick) [2]... in September, but last year the crops (not harvest) [3]... until August and the apples and pears (not/pick) [4]... until October. Because the weather was so mild in the autumn, the horses (leave) [5]... outside in the fields until early December; normally they (bring) [6]... inside at the beginning of November.

Vocabulary

5 Rewrite the sentences using a form or a phrase with *get* in place of the words in *italics*.

She *achieved* very good results at university.
She got very good results at university.

1 Could you *fetch* some milk from the fridge?
2 I *received* a cheque for £50 in the post this morning.
3 What time does the train *arrive in* Falmouth?
4 My sister *became* quite nervous just before the interview for the job.
5 I want to *change my clothes* before I go out again.
6 Did you know that Sam and Lucy *had their wedding ceremony* in Mauritius?

6 Choose the odd word in each group.

polite	friendly	<u>rude</u>	helpful
1 wrist	knee	elbow	shoulder
2 claw	wing	feather	ear
3 smell	peck	flap	fly
4 veal	chicken	lamb	beef

Communication

7 Reorder the sentences to complete the conversation in a restaurant.

A: *Excuse me.*

a) I'm afraid this chicken isn't cooked properly.
b) Yes, can I help you?
c) I don't think so but I'll tell them to do it straightaway.
d) Thanks very much. Will it take long?
e) I'm sorry about that. I'll ask them to cook it a bit longer.

13 ▶ If I had the money, ...

Learning goals

Communication
Talk about imaginary situations in the future
Ask for and give advice

Grammar
Pronouns: *some-, any-, no-,
every-* + *thing, one, where*
Second conditional: *if* clause + *'d
(would)/wouldn't*

Vocabulary
Personality adjectives:
sensitive, aggressive, etc.

Your hopes, dreams and ambitions

Mel, 16, is American and lives in North Dakota in the USA.

Amy, 15, is British and lives in Cardiff, in South Wales.

If you could go anywhere in the world, which country would you go to?

Amy: I'd go to the USA – anywhere in the USA. I've always wanted to go there since I was a kid. My brother has been there but I haven't. I'd love to see the Grand Canyon and go to San Francisco. The USA would be my first choice. My second choice would be somewhere exotic like Japan or Indonesia.

Mel: I'd go to the Far East, to somewhere like Thailand. I'd really like to get to know another culture and Thailand sounds so different from the USA. I'd like to live there for a bit if I could.

Before you read

Look at the items in the chart in Exercise 1 and think about your dreams and ambitions.

1> Read

a> Read about Amy and Mel's dreams and complete the chart.

	Amy	Mel
Country to visit: Famous person to meet: Item to buy: Things about appearance they'd like to change: Social changes to make:		

b> Are any of Amy and Mel's dreams and ambitions the same as yours? Tell the class.

Grammar flash

Pronouns: *some-, any-, no-, every-* **+** *thing, one, where*

a) What are the missing words?

	some-	any-	no-	every-
Place:	somewhere	...	nowhere	...
Object:	...	anything	...	everything
Person:	someone	...	no one	...
	...	anybody	...	everybody

Note
Words ending in *-one* and *-body* mean the same, i.e. *someone = somebody.*

b) Go back and look.
Which of the pronouns can you find in Exercise 1?

2> Practice

Complete the passage with words from the Grammar flash.

Fed up with town!

❛I'm fed up with my town. There is ¹ *nothing* to do in the evening and ² ... to go. I think ³ ... should build a sports centre or ⁴ ... like that. After all, ⁵ ... likes sports, or at least most people do. There are lots of places for the over 21s to go but there isn't ⁶ ... for teenagers like us. It would be really nice to be able to go ⁷ ... after school to meet friends, listen to music and have ⁸ ... to eat and drink. The trouble is that ⁹ ... costs so much in the cafés in town. It's stupid to charge £1.50 for a coke. ¹⁰ ... wants to spend that sort of money on a drink, for goodness' sake!❜

If you could meet a famous person, who would you choose?

Amy: I'd choose Julia Roberts. She's a good actress. She was brilliant in her last film.

Mel: I think I'd choose Jim Carrey. I think he's really funny. I love his films.

If someone gave you £500, what would you buy?

Amy: I'd buy a new music system and some CDs.

Mel: I'd probably buy a new mountain bike because I live in mountain country in North Dakota and it would be really great to go out at weekends with my friends. I might buy some computer games too.

If you could, what would you change about your appearance?

Amy: I'd like to be taller and I'd like to have long dark hair.

Mel: I wouldn't change anything. I'm happy with the way I am.

If you were prime minister or president, what would you change first?

Mel: I'd build more homes for the homeless.

Amy: I think I'd do something about schools. I'd make sure that all schools had good teachers and I'd give schools more money, because people need a good education to get a job.

Grammar snapshot

Second conditional: *if* clause + *'d (would)/wouldn't*

If clause	Main clause
If I had the money,	I'**d (would)** go to Japan.
If I were you,	I'**d (would)** buy a mountain bike.
If he *could** drive,	he'**d (would)** buy a car.
If someone gave them £1,000,	they **wouldn't** buy a car.
If I didn't have a bike,	I **wouldn't** be able to go and see my friends.

Notes
1. The second conditional is used to talk about unreal or unlikely situations or to give advice.
2. *If I were you* is more common than *If I was you.*
3. *could* is the past tense of *can* in this case.

a) Make a rule.
In the second conditional, the verb in the *if* clause is always in the ... tense.

b) What's the difference in meaning?
1. If I have the money, I'll buy a bike.
2. If I had the money, I'd buy a bike.

3 〉 Practice

Complete the conversation using the second conditional.

A: What (you/do) ¹*would you do* if you (have) ²*had* a lot of money?
B: You mean, what (I/do) ³... if I (win) ⁴... the lottery or something?
A: Yes, how (you spend) ⁵... it?
B: If I (win) ⁶... more than £10,000, I (save) ⁷... it.
A: But if you (not/win) ⁸... very much, say, if it (be) ⁹... only £1,000?
B: I (go) ¹⁰... on holiday or buy a music system. What (you/do) ¹¹... ?
A: I (not/waste) ¹²... money on a holiday. I (buy) ¹³... the latest computer.
B: (you/give) ¹⁴... any of it to charity?
A: Yes, I ¹⁵... . Some of it!

4 〉 Over to you

Interview your partner with the questions from the text in Exercise 1.

A: *If you could go anywhere in the world, which country would you go to?*
B: *I'd go to India.*
A: *Why?*
B: *Because I've always wanted to see the Taj Mahal.*

Tell the class about your partner.

5 〉 Writing helpline

Check written work

Always leave time to check your written work and ask yourself questions like:
1. Have I missed out any words?
2. Is the spelling correct?
3. What about the grammar?
4. Is it punctuated correctly with commas, full stops and question marks?

Ask a friend to read it afterwards.

6 〉 Write

Write your own answers to the interview questions from the text in Exercise 1.

7 〉 ⋯ Listen

Listen to a radio programme in which Helen and Phil talk about things they would put in a time capsule. Copy the chart and make notes.

	Helen	Phil
Music: Book: Personal item:		

8 Over to you

Think about your ideal partner and then answer Y (Yes) or N (No) to find out about yourself.

Perfect partners?

1 Would you prefer your partner to be quiet and sensible rather than loud and outgoing?

2 If a boyfriend/girlfriend said 'I love you' on your first date, would you run a mile?

3 If your partner flirted with someone at a party, would you be upset?

4 Would you expect your partner to cheer you up if you felt depressed?

5 Would you refuse to go out with someone very popular and good-looking if you didn't have the same interests?

6 If your boyfriend/girlfriend wanted to kiss you on your first date, would you refuse?

7 Would you be upset if you had a row with your partner?

8 If your partner told you that he/she didn't like your friends, would you finish with him/her?

9 Would you prefer your partner to be your 'best' friend rather than someone who you just like going out with?

10 If your partner told a lie about something unimportant, would you forgive them?

KEY

If you answered 'Yes' more than 7 times:
You are very sensible about the people you choose to go out with. You are quite romantic but you like to get to know someone before you get serious about them. Sometimes you may be too serious.

If you answered 'Yes' 5–7 times:
You are very sociable and friendly. You are emotional when you need to be but you don't let your feelings run away with you. However, you may sometimes do things you regret later on.

If you answered mostly 'No':
You are very sociable and you change partners quite frequently. You don't take relationships very seriously. This may cause you problems in the future.

9 Vocabulary

Personality adjectives

• emotional • bossy • serious • lighthearted • loud
• outgoing • practical • quick-tempered • quiet • reliable
• romantic • shy • sensitive • sociable • aggressive

a Which of these adjectives do you think describe you?

b In pairs, use the adjectives to talk about yourself and the personalities of people you like and don't like.

I'm a bit shy, so I like people who are sociable and outgoing. I don't like people who are loud or aggressive.

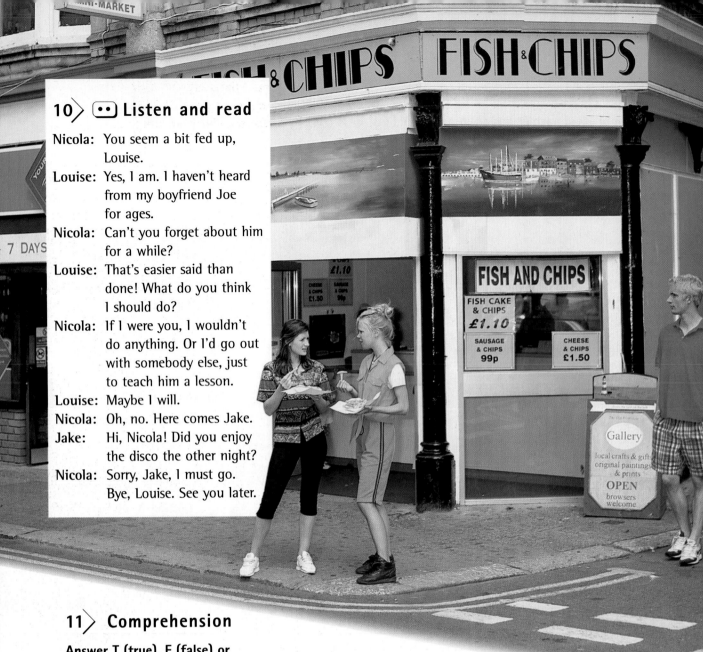

10 🔊 Listen and read

Nicola: You seem a bit fed up, Louise.

Louise: Yes, I am. I haven't heard from my boyfriend Joe for ages.

Nicola: Can't you forget about him for a while?

Louise: That's easier said than done! What do you think I should do?

Nicola: If I were you, I wouldn't do anything. Or I'd go out with somebody else, just to teach him a lesson.

Louise: Maybe I will.

Nicola: Oh, no. Here comes Jake.

Jake: Hi, Nicola! Did you enjoy the disco the other night?

Nicola: Sorry, Jake, I must go. Bye, Louise. See you later.

11 Comprehension

Answer T (true), F (false) or DK (don't know).

1 Louise is in a good mood.
2 Joe has been away for three days.
3 Nicola tells Louise not to think about Joe so much.
4 Louise still likes Joe a lot.
5 Nicola is pleased to see Jake.

12 🔊 Useful phrases

Listen and repeat.

- You seem a bit fed up.
- That's easier said than done.
- Just to teach him a lesson.

13 🔊 Soundbite

Intonation of conditionals

If I were you, I wouldn't do anything.
(Look at page 123.)

14 Communication

Asking for and giving advice

▶ I've found a £20 note in the street. What do you think I should do?
▶ If I were you, I'd keep it.
▶ I can't do that.
▶ Well, why don't you hand it in to the police?
▶ Yes, that's a good idea./Yes, all right./Yes, I suppose so./Mm. I'm not sure.

In pairs, make similar conversations in these situations. Use the ideas in brackets, then give some more advice of your own.

- Your best friend has arranged to go to the cinema with you but another friend has just invited you to a birthday party. (go to the party)
- You have promised to visit your sick grandmother in hospital on Saturday afternoon but there is an exciting football match on television at the same time. (watch the match)
- You have been getting unpleasant phone calls from a stranger. (ask your parents to change your telephone number)
- You borrowed a cassette from a friend two weeks ago but now you have lost it. (keep quiet about it)

Suspicious behaviour

Read the story and try to guess the missing words. Then listen and see if you were right.

So you wouldn't go out with Jake again even if ____ you?

____ !

But ____ ?

He talked about ____ for half the evening and danced with ____ for the other half.

2 You're too ____ . That's your problem.

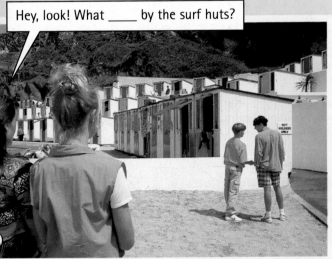

Hey, look! What ____ by the surf huts?

Are you looking for anyone special? I ____ if I were you.

Yes, that's private property. It belongs to the surf club.

4

What's ____ ?

It's surfing equipment. It's nothing to do with you.

Sounds interesting.

Yeah, right. Interesting.

6

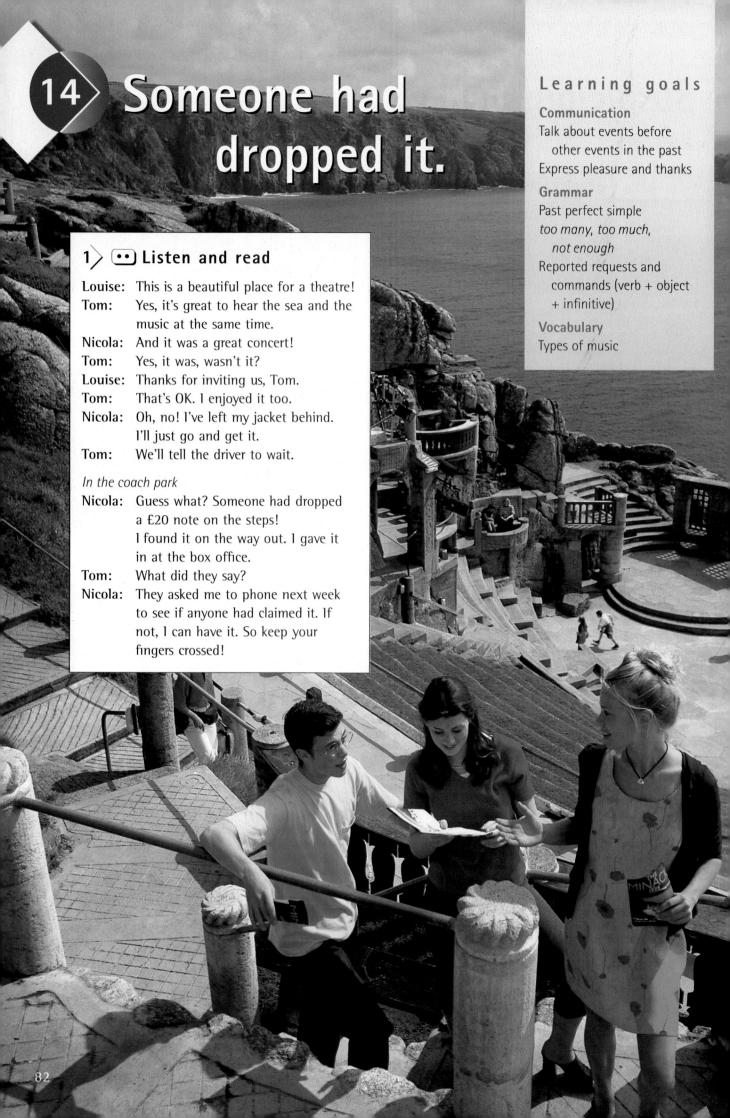

14 ▷ Someone had dropped it.

Learning goals

Communication
Talk about events before
  other events in the past
Express pleasure and thanks

Grammar
Past perfect simple
*too many, too much,
  not enough*
Reported requests and
  commands (verb + object
  + infinitive)

Vocabulary
Types of music

1> ⊡ Listen and read

Louise: This is a beautiful place for a theatre!

Tom: Yes, it's great to hear the sea and the music at the same time.

Nicola: And it was a great concert!

Tom: Yes, it was, wasn't it?

Louise: Thanks for inviting us, Tom.

Tom: That's OK. I enjoyed it too.

Nicola: Oh, no! I've left my jacket behind. I'll just go and get it.

Tom: We'll tell the driver to wait.

In the coach park

Nicola: Guess what? Someone had dropped a £20 note on the steps! I found it on the way out. I gave it in at the box office.

Tom: What did they say?

Nicola: They asked me to phone next week to see if anyone had claimed it. If not, I can have it. So keep your fingers crossed!

82

2 Comprehension

Put the events in the correct order.

1d) Tom, Nicola and Louise arrive at the Minack Theatre for a concert.

a) Nicola finds the £20 note.
b) The box office tell her to phone the following week.
c) Nicola goes back to get her jacket.
d) Tom, Nicola and Louise arrive at the Minack Theatre for a concert.
e) Nicola hands the money in at the box office.
f) The concert ends and Nicola realises she has forgotten her jacket.

3 👀 Useful phrases

Listen and repeat.

- I've left [my jacket] behind.
- Guess what?
- Keep your fingers crossed!

Grammar snapshot

Past perfect simple

Positive statements
She'd (had) left her jacket behind.

Negative statements
She **hadn't remembered** to pick it up.

a) Look at the sentences. Which happens first, 'feeling better' or 'eating the meal'?
1 I felt better because I'd eaten a good meal.
2 I felt better so I ate a good meal.

b) Make a rule.
1 We use the past perfect simple tense to describe an event in the past that happened ... another event in the past.

4 Practice

Match the openings with the correct endings to make sentences. Use the verb in brackets in the past perfect or the past simple.

1c) Louise had arrived at the hotel a few days before Nicola started work.

1 Louise (arrive) at the hotel a few days
2 Nicola (know) Newquay quite well
3 Louise (not/be) to the Minack Theatre
4 Rick Ward (begin) to bully Jamie
5 After the concert Nicola (realise) that
6 Nicola (not/can) find

a) before Tom (take) them there.
b) she (forget) her jacket.
c) before Nicola (start) work.
d) the person who (drop) the £20 note.
e) because she (be) there before.
f) several weeks before Jamie (tell) Tom.

First time at a festival

When 16-year-old Rachel Pointer saw the advertisement for the Glastonbury pop festival, she really wanted to go.

'My friends Sally and Jacky had been to the festival the year before. They said it was great and they really wanted to go again. The trouble was Dad didn't want me to go so I asked Mum to talk to him. Actually, I don't think that either of my parents were very happy about it but they changed their minds when I told them that my cousin Rob, who is 21, was going to go with us. Before I went, Mum had a chat with me about the sort of things that can happen at pop festivals and I told her not to worry.

Anyway, we all took the train to Glastonbury on Wednesday and I rang Dad from the station when we got there. He wanted me to ring every day but I said that wasn't possible as there were too many people queuing for the phones. He wasn't very pleased about that so in the end I agreed to phone him again on Saturday.

We put up our tents in one of the fields. Of course, I had taken too many clothes and too much food. There were food stalls everywhere. The music was great but, in fact, we didn't see very many bands. We sat around and talked a lot – after all you don't go to a pop festival just for the music. You go to meet people and have fun. I made about twenty new friends in the four days that I was there, including two really nice girls from Italy. The people there were from all over the world.

Dad picked us up from the station when we got back on Sunday night. I think he had been quite worried about us but it wasn't dangerous at the festival. There were far too many security people there for anything bad to happen. I'll definitely go again next year if my parents let me.'

Before you read

Have you ever been to a pop festival? Would you like to go to one?

5> Reading helpline

Skimreading

When you first look at a reading text, it is a good idea to skim through it quickly to note any names, places and dates. These will help you to get an idea of who and what the text is about, and when and where it is set.

6> Read

a> Skimread the article and find:

1 the name of the event   2 people's names
3 people's ages   4 days of the week   5 a country.

b> Read the article again and answer the questions.

1 Why did Rachel want to go to the festival?
2 What did her parents think of the idea?
3 What made them change their minds?
4 What did Rachel's mother talk to her about?
5 Why was it difficult for Rachel to phone her father?
6 Apart from listening to music, how did Rachel and her friends spend most of the time?
7 Were there only English people at the festival?
8 Why didn't Rachel feel the festival was dangerous?

7> Discussion

Would your parents allow you to go to a pop festival? Why? / Why not?

8> Memory bank

Types of music

a> List as many different types of music as you can in two minutes.

b> Choose your favourite from your list. Then find the most popular types of music in your group.

Grammar flash

too many, too much, not enough
I didn't enjoy the party because:
• there were **too many** people there.
• there was **too much** soft rock.
• there was**n't enough** food.
• there were**n't enough** crisps.

Make a rule about countable and uncountable nouns.
We use *too many* with ... nouns, *too much* with ... and *(not) enough* with ... and ... nouns.

9 > Practice

Rephrase the comments about a pop festival, using *too much*, *too many* or *not enough*.

There were too many people.

1 There were so many people that we could hardly move.
2 There was a lot of soft rock, which I don't like.
3 There was no room to pitch our tents.
4 There were only twelve toilets! Disgusting!
5 How many old rock groups from the 1980s were there? At least six!
6 We took lots of food. We only ate half of it.

Grammar snapshot

Reported requests and commands

Positive	Negative
He wanted me to go.	He **didn't** want me to go.
He asked him to leave.	He asked him **not** to leave.
He told her to hurry.	He told her **not** to hurry.

10 Practice

a) Say what Rachel's parents *asked/wanted/told* **her to do when she got home. Use the cues below.**

1 My mother asked me not to bring my sleeping bag inside.

1 My mother/ask/not bring my sleeping bag inside.
2 She/tell/have a shower and wash my hair.
3 My father/tell/not use the phone all evening.
4 They/ask/go with them to visit my grandmother.
5 My mother/not want/play my new CDs.
6 My father/want/do my holiday essay.

b) Talk about some of the things that your parents have recently asked or told you to do or not to do.

My mother told me not to play my music so loudly.
I didn't agree with her but I turned the sound down a little.

11 Soundbite Sentence stress

He <u>told</u> us to <u>stop</u>.   (Look at page 123.)

12 Listen

Listen to Tessa describing Glastonbury Festival and answer the questions.

1 What does Tessa say about:
   a) the tents?   b) the food?
   c) the age range?   d) security checks?
   e) the cost?   f) the fences?
   g) number of people?   h) the toilets?
2 What makes the festival special?
3 What's her opinion of it in general?

13 Write

Write a paragraph describing the incident at the fence which Tessa talked about.

14 Communication

Expressing pleasure and thanks

In informal situations

▶ That was a great concert/an interesting film!
▶ Yes, it was, wasn't it?
▶ Thanks for inviting me/suggesting it.
▶ That's OK. I enjoyed it too.

In more formal situations

▶ Thank you for a lovely evening/lunch/ barbecue/party. I had a really nice time.
▶ You're welcome. I'm glad you could come.
▶ So am I. It was very nice to talk to you/see you again.

In pairs, make similar conversations in these situations. Then invent further situations of your own.

1 An English teacher invites you to a barbecue. You enjoy it very much.

2 A friend lends you her new All Saints album which you think is great.

3 A Canadian teacher invites your class out on a picnic. You think he is very interesting to talk to.

Fast rewind UNITS 13 and 14

Grammar

1 **Complete the text with the past continuous or past perfect form of the verbs.**

New York story

Last year my uncle (work) [1] *was working* in the USA and he and my aunt (decide) [2] *had decided* to spend a few days in New York. One day they (walk) [3] ... down the street when a young man suddenly bumped into my uncle. My uncle noticed that his shoulder (drip) [4] ... with tomato ketchup! A young girl, who (stand) [5] ... beside him, began to wipe his jacket. Luckily, my aunt, who (see) [6] ... everything, shouted: 'John! Watch out!' The young girl quickly disappeared. Then my uncle realised that he (nearly/be) [7] ... the victim of a clever pair of pickpockets.

2 **Make second conditional sentences using the verbs in brackets.**

If you (train) harder, you (get) into the team.
If you trained harder, you'd get into the team.

1 If I (be) you, I (tell) the truth.
2 Where (you/like) to live if you (can) choose anywhere?
3 If you (not/stay up) so late, you (not/feel) so tired.
4 I (not/be) late for school so often if you (give) me a lift.
5 What (your father/say) if he (walk) into the room now?
6 I (be) so happy if I (win) some money on the lottery.

3 **Complete the sentences with a pronoun:** *some-, any-, no-, every- + one,* **where** or *thing.*

Is there *anyone* here who can speak Russian?

1 Where are my sunglasses? They must be ... .
2 I can't believe it. The place is empty. There's ... here!
3 Where's Kerry? She's ... to be seen.
4 Hello. Is there ... at home?
5 I've prepared ... to eat but it's ... special.
6 Oh no! Turn the tap off! There's water ... !
7 I haven't got ... to wear.
8 She adores her boyfriend. He means ... to her.

4 **Complete the conversation with** *too many, too much* **or** *not enough.*

A: Let's go swimming at the Lido pool this afternoon.
B: No, I've had [1] *too much* lunch. And there are always [2] ... people at the Lido in the afternoon.
A: Oh, don't be so boring!
B: Anyway, I've got [3] ... homework to do.
A: You can do it later before we go to the cinema.
B: No, there's [4] ... time. I'm off. Bye!

5 **Report the following using the past simple of the verb in brackets.**

'Could you close the door?' he said to her. (ask)
He asked her to close the door.

1 'Put your bags in the car!' he said to me. (tell)
2 'Don't wait for me, ' she said to him. (tell)
3 'Please don't tell my parents,' she said to us. (ask)
4 'Can you look at my essay?' he said to her. (want)
5 'Could you move up a bit?' she said to them. (ask)
6 'Please don't play my CDs without asking,' she said to him. (want)

Vocabulary

6 **Complete the sentences with** *say* **or** *tell.*

He *told* me all about the accident.

1 How do you ... 'Goodbye' in Japanese?
2 I want you to ... me the truth!
3 Please don't ... anything to my mother about the vase.
4 My sister likes me to ... her a story at bed time.
5 Could you ... me the time, please?

Communication

7 **Work in pairs. Student A:**

You have just spent the weekend at Student B's house.
• Say how great you thought the weekend was.
• Thank B for inviting you.
• Ask B for advice on what to buy his/her parents to say thank you.

Now Student B:

It is your birthday. Student A has given you a CD. You are planning to go out to a club with A in the evening.
• Thank A for the CD.
• Say how much you like it.
• Ask A for advice on what to say to his/her parents about going out that evening.

Progress update Units 13 and 14

How do you rate your progress? Tick the chart.

	Excellent ★★★★	Good ★★★	OK ★★	Can do better ★
Grammar				
Vocabulary				
Communication				

A CIRCUS WITH A DIFFERENCE

If you mention the circus to most people, they think of animals which are made to do tricks and are kept in cages. The *Cirque du Soleil* is very different. The performers are not animals. They are all human.

Audiences everywhere are enthralled by the performers at *Cirque du Soleil*. These amazing acrobats do more than just swing on trapezes: they bungee jump; they swing up, down and around Chinese poles; and they contort their bodies in amazing ways. People come from far and wide to see their show.

Cirque du Soleil began in 1984 when two French-Canadian street-performers, Gilles Ste-Croix, a stilt-walker, and Guy Laliberte, a fire-eater, decided to form a circus without animals. They made up a troupe with people from all over the world. Tight-wire artist Wang Jing-min is Chinese, Rene Bazinet is a clown from Germany, and the Lorador brothers, who do a brilliant hand-balancing act, are from Portugal. During the performance of the current show, nine different languages are spoken backstage.

For the show's young performers the circus is their life. Laurence Racine, a seventeen-year-old French girl, is a contortionist who has been in the circus since the age of eleven. Her mother used to travel with the circus as a wardrobe assistant when Laurence first started, but now Laurence is on her own. Laurence misses her family but she has made many friends in the circus. 'We are like a big friendly family because we grew up together. We train together, perform together, even eat together and share rooms. It's all very intense.'

Laurence performs an amazing acrobatic act with three other girls. 'It may look simple,' says Laurence, 'but we have practised for six years to get it absolutely right. In the circus, you won't succeed unless you are both physically and mentally strong.'

Laurence, who looks younger than her seventeen years, is not excluded from education or exams. In fact she has school lessons for six hours a day. 'But I feel that I have grown up very fast in the circus. Friends at home who are the same age as me are waiting for their lives to begin, but I feel that I have already done a lot with my life. I've travelled all over the world and I'm doing something I really enjoy. I wouldn't want to do anything else, even if I had the chance. My life may not appear normal to other teenagers, but it's normal to me and I love it.'

Before you read

Have you ever been to a circus? If so, where was it and what was it like? Did you enjoy it?

1 Read

Read about the *Cirque du Soleil* **and answer the questions.**

1 When was the *Cirque du Soleil* founded?
2 Who were its founders? Where do they come from?
3 What is the unique feature of the circus?
4 What nationality is the tight-wire artist?
5 What does Rene Bazinet do?
6 Who does a hand-balancing act?
7 What does Laurence Racine do? Who with?
8 How long has Laurence been with the circus?

2 Speak

Prepare questions for an interview between a journalist and Laurence Racine. Roleplay the interview in pairs.

A: *How old are you?*
B: *I'm seventeen.*
A: *What do you do in the circus?*

3 ☺ Listen

Listen to an interview with Michael, one of the troupe's youngest performers, and answer the questions.

1 What does he do in the circus?
2 How long has he been there?
3 What is a typical day like for him?
4 What famous people has he met?

4 Write

Write a letter to a friend describing Michael's life with the circus. Use your notes from Exercise 3.

Dear Joanne,
I have just met a very interesting person. He's a circus star. At the moment he … .

5 Discussion

Are performing animals popular in circuses in your country?
Are animals used anywhere else in public to amuse people?
Do you think performing animals are happy?
If you had the power, would you stop the use of animals for entertainment?

Project ▶ ③ Snapshot of food and drink

A ▶ How a food or drink product is made

Choose a food or drink product which you like or consume every day and describe how it is made. Find pictures to illustrate your project.

Where does the product come from?

Chocolate is produced from the seeds ('beans') which are inside the pods of cocoa trees. It

Where is it grown or produced?

Cocoa trees are grown in areas of the world which have wet, tropical climates, like central Africa and parts of the Caribbean and Latin

How is it produced?

Cocoa beans don't taste like chocolate. To make chocolate, farmers add water to the beans and wrap them in banana leaves to ferment for six days. Then they are left to dry in the sun. This creates the chocolate flavour. The cocoa beans are then roasted and ground into a thick brown liquid. Milk, cream, sugar and flavouring are added and beaten many times to create the mixture which is used in chocolate bars and

B ▶ Daily diet

Write a project about two people's daily diet. Interview them and list what each person eats in a day.

Interview 1: What Craig eats in a typical day

Breakfast:	Cornflakes with milk, two slices of toast and jam
Lunch:	A cheese and tomato ketchup sandwich
Dinner:	Chicken and rice
Snacks:	A milk chocolate bar and some sweets
Drinks:	Coffee

Say if the diet is healthy or not.

This is not a very healthy diet. Doctors recommend that we should eat five portions of fresh fruit and vegetables a day, but Craig

Make some recommendations.

It would be a good idea if Craig

3 Take a break

This song was written by John Lennon and Paul McCartney. It featured in the Beatles' album, *Sergeant Pepper's Lonely Hearts Club Band*, which was released in June 1967.

When I'm sixty-four

When I get older ¹*losing my hair*,
many years from now.
Will you still be sending me a Valentine,
birthday greetings, bottle of wine?
If I'd been out till ².............. ,
would you lock the door?
Will you still need me, will you still feed me,
when I'm sixty-four?
³.............. too,
and if you say the word,
I could stay with you.
I could be handy, mending a fuse
when your lights have gone.
You can knit a sweater by the fireside,
Sunday mornings ⁴.............. .
Doing the garden, digging the weeds,
⁵.............. ?
Will you still need me, will you still feed me,
when I'm sixty-four?
Every summer we can ⁶.............. ,
in the Isle of Wight, if it's not too dear,
we shall scrimp and save.
Grandchildren ⁷.............. ,
Vera, Chuck and Dave.
⁸.............. , drop me a line,
stating point of view.
Indicate precisely what you ⁹.............. ,
yours sincerely, wasting away.
Give me your answer, ¹⁰.............. ,
mine for ever more.
Will you still need me, will you still feed me,
when I'm sixty-four?

1> 👀' Listen and complete the lyrics of the song. Then check at the back of the book and see if you were right.

2> Find words or phrases in the song which mean the same as the following.

• going bald • expensive • live carefully and not waste money • send me a letter • opinion
• exactly • always

3> In what ways are your grandparents like or different from the people in the song?

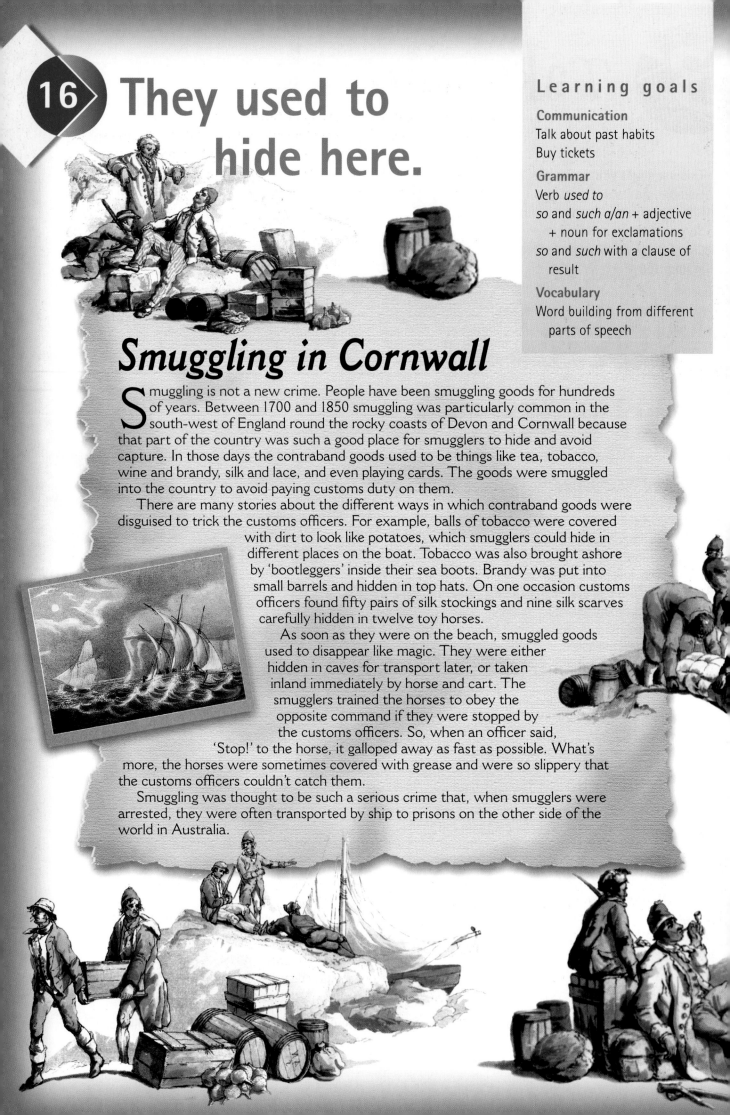

16 ▸ They used to hide here.

Learning goals

Communication
Talk about past habits
Buy tickets

Grammar
Verb *used to*
so and *such a/an* + adjective
   + noun for exclamations
so and *such* with a clause of
   result

Vocabulary
Word building from different
   parts of speech

Smuggling in Cornwall

Smuggling is not a new crime. People have been smuggling goods for hundreds of years. Between 1700 and 1850 smuggling was particularly common in the south-west of England round the rocky coasts of Devon and Cornwall because that part of the country was such a good place for smugglers to hide and avoid capture. In those days the contraband goods used to be things like tea, tobacco, wine and brandy, silk and lace, and even playing cards. The goods were smuggled into the country to avoid paying customs duty on them.

There are many stories about the different ways in which contraband goods were disguised to trick the customs officers. For example, balls of tobacco were covered with dirt to look like potatoes, which smugglers could hide in different places on the boat. Tobacco was also brought ashore by 'bootleggers' inside their sea boots. Brandy was put into small barrels and hidden in top hats. On one occasion customs officers found fifty pairs of silk stockings and nine silk scarves carefully hidden in twelve toy horses.

As soon as they were on the beach, smuggled goods used to disappear like magic. They were either hidden in caves for transport later, or taken inland immediately by horse and cart. The smugglers trained the horses to obey the opposite command if they were stopped by the customs officers. So, when an officer said, 'Stop!' to the horse, it galloped away as fast as possible. What's more, the horses were sometimes covered with grease and were so slippery that the customs officers couldn't catch them.

Smuggling was thought to be such a serious crime that, when smugglers were arrested, they were often transported by ship to prisons on the other side of the world in Australia.

1 > Read

a > Read and guess the meaning of these words.

- goods • capture (*n.*) • contraband • lace • duty • disguise (*v.*)
- trick (*v.*) • customs officer • cover (*v.*) • dirt • bootlegger
- barrel • top hat • disappear • obey • command (*n.*) • gallop
- grease • slippery • arrest • transport (*v.*)

b > Answer T (true) or F (false).

1 The rocky coast of south-west England was ideal for smuggling.
2 Smuggling declined in England after 1850.
3 People only smuggled tobacco and brandy.
4 Smugglers made balls of tobacco which looked like potatoes.
5 Smugglers used specially trained horses to trick the customs officers.
6 Smuggling was seen as an unimportant crime.

2 > Discussion

How common is smuggling today?
What sort of things do people smuggle?
Is it a serious crime?
What are the problems involved in catching smugglers today?

3 > Vocabulary

Word building from different parts of speech

Verb	Verbal noun (gerund *-ing* form)	Noun (*-er/-or*)
smuggle	smuggling	smuggler

a > Copy the three headings and put the different parts of speech of these verbs under the correct headings.

- paint • cook • act • drive • heat • build • sing

b > Answer the questions.

In which two words:
1 is the *-ing* form both an activity and a separate noun?
2 is the *-er* noun not a person?

4 > Practice

**Complete the sentences using the words from Exercise 3
in the correct form.**

1 One of Van Gogh's most famous ... is of a vase of sunflowers.
2 My Mum wants a new ... for her kitchen.
3 Could you turn the central ... on for me, please?
4 He's such a bad ... he's had quite a lot of accidents.
5 Who's going to do the ... for supper?
6 She's got a good voice so she's interested in ... and ... .
7 We need a ... to repair the roof of our house.
8 You can warm the room with this electric ... .

5 🔊 Listen and read

Tom, Louise and Nicola are visiting a Cornish fishing village.

Nicola: Let's go on a boat trip.

Louise: But it's late. It's already four o'clock.

Nicola: Oh, come on, Louise. Don't be so boring! It's such a nice day.

Louise: Oh, all right.

Tom: Excuse me. What time's the next boat trip?

Man: At four fifteen.

Nicola: Did Mousehole use to be a fishing port?

Man: Yes, it did. It used to be very busy but things have changed now.

Tom: What happened?

Man: There used to be more fish in the sea.

Louise: Really?

Man: Yes. Most of the fish have gone now, partly because of pollution and partly because of over-fishing. You're only allowed to fish on certain days now.

Nicola: So how do people make a living?

Man: From tourism. I take tourists round the coast in my boat and show them places where the smugglers used to hide their goods.

Tom: Were smugglers very common round here?

Man: They certainly were. I'll show you some of their secret hiding places during the trip.

6 Comprehension

Complete the sentences.

1 At first Louise doesn't want to take a boat trip because ...

2 Not long ago the boat was ...

3 Mousehole was known in the past as a ...

4 There aren't so many fish in the sea now because ... and because ...

5 The man takes tourists round the coast in his boat to ...

7 🔊 Useful phrases

Listen and repeat.

- Don't be so boring!
- Things have changed.
- Partly because of [...].
- They certainly were.

94

Grammar snapshot

Verb *used to*

Positive statements
It **used to** be a fishing port (but it isn't now).

Negative statements
It did**n't use to** be a pleasure boat (but it is now).

Question
Did it **use to** be a fishing port (in the past)?

We use *used to* to talk about things which were true in the past but are not true now.

What's the difference in meaning?
1 He took me out in his fishing boat.
2 He used to take me out in his fishing boat.

8〉 Practice

a〉 Look at the pictures on the right and rephrase their captions with *used to*.

1 Cornish people used to speak their own language.

b〉 Use the cues to ask and answer questions.

1 A: *Did they always use to speak English in Cornwall?*
   B: *No, they didn't. They used to speak their own language.*

1 always/speak English in Cornwall?
2 ever/trade overseas?
3 mining/be an important industry?
4 treat/children well?
5 early visitors/come to Newquay for the scenery?
6 fishermen/catch a lot of tuna fish?

9〉 Over to you

Talk about life in your country in the past.

1 Where did people use to live?
2 How did they use to make a living?
3 How did people use to dress?
4 What did they use to eat and drink?
5 How did they use to spend their free time?

10〉 Write

Write about the way your parents or grandparents used to live.

Cornwall in the past

PYSK / FISH

GWEDHEN / TREE

1 Once upon a time Cornish people spoke their own language.

2 In early times Cornish people traded all over the Roman Empire.

3 In the seventeenth and eighteenth centuries Cornwall produced most of the world's tin and copper.

4 It was common for children to work down the tin mines.

5 In the nineteenth century visitors came to Newquay for health reasons.

6 Pilchards were once the main catch for Cornish fishermen.

11 > Communication

Buying tickets

▶ Can I have three tickets for the boat trip, please?
▶ Certainly.
▶ How much are they?
▶ Five pounds each. That's fifteen pounds altogether.
▶ Fifteen pounds! Is it cheaper for students?

▶ No, sorry. It's the same price for everyone. Only children under ten are half price.

▶ Yes, it's half price but I need to see your student cards.
▶ I'm afraid we haven't got them with us.
▶ Sorry! But I have to see them.

In pairs, roleplay the following situations.

1 **Student B:** Turn to page 121.
   Student A: You work part-time at the ticket office at the Tate Gallery. Entry to the special exhibition is £6. Student rate is £4. (Students must show student cards.)

2 **Student B:** Turn to page 121.
   Student A: You are in London and want to see the musical *West Side Story*. You go to the theatre box office. Find out if there are special rates for students on weekday nights. You have only got your passport with you.

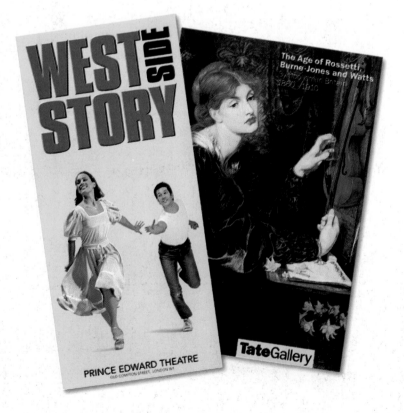

Grammar flash

so + **adjective**
Don't be **so** boring!

such (*a/an*) + **adjective** + **noun**
It was **such a** good/**such an** easy place to hide.
They're **such** nice boats.

so and *such* with a clause of result
The horses were **so** slippery **that** they couldn't catch them.
Smuggling was **such a** serious crime **that** smugglers were transported to Australia.

Note: *that* can be omitted.

12 > Practice

Complete the sentences with *so* or *such a/an* and an appropriate word from this list.

• angry • cold • expensive • lovely
• loud • beautiful • late

1 It was such a lovely day that we went for a swim.

1 It was ... day that we went for a swim.
2 Ssh! Don't speak in ... voice. Someone will hear us.
3 Nicola was ... that she slammed the door as she left.
4 I'm ... that I can't stop to talk.
5 The trouble with organic food is that it's ... .
6 I like Florence. It's ... city.
7 The weather was ... yesterday I had to wear a warm coat.

13 > 😊 Soundbite

Emphatic stress with *so* and *such*

<u>so</u> **tired**   <u>such</u> **a cold day**
(Look at page 123.)

14 > 😊 Listen

Ben's mother has got an old snapshot of him. Listen to the conversation. How has Ben changed?

(West Side Story — Prince Edward Theatre. The Age of Rossetti, Burne-Jones and Watts — Tate Gallery.)

Bad news

Read the story and try to guess the missing words. Then listen and see if you were right.

Can I have a copy, please? _____ ?

It's free. It's full of all the latest surfing news.

A break-in at the surf hut. Oh, no! I hope _____ . I'd better go and find out.

BAD NEWS FOR VISITING SURF TEAM

2

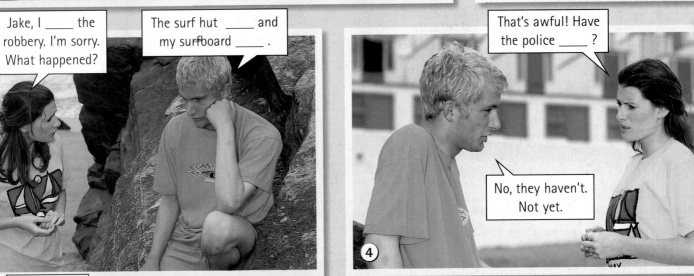

Jake, I _____ the robbery. I'm sorry. What happened?

The surf hut _____ and my surfboard _____ .

That's awful! Have the police _____ ?

No, they haven't. Not yet.

4

I wonder ... .

...ell, the other day _____ and ...ey looked a bit suspicious.

You wonder what?

Would you recognise them if _____ ?

_____.

I can't believe it. Newquay used to be a nice, safe place.

Yes, it's the same everywhere.

6

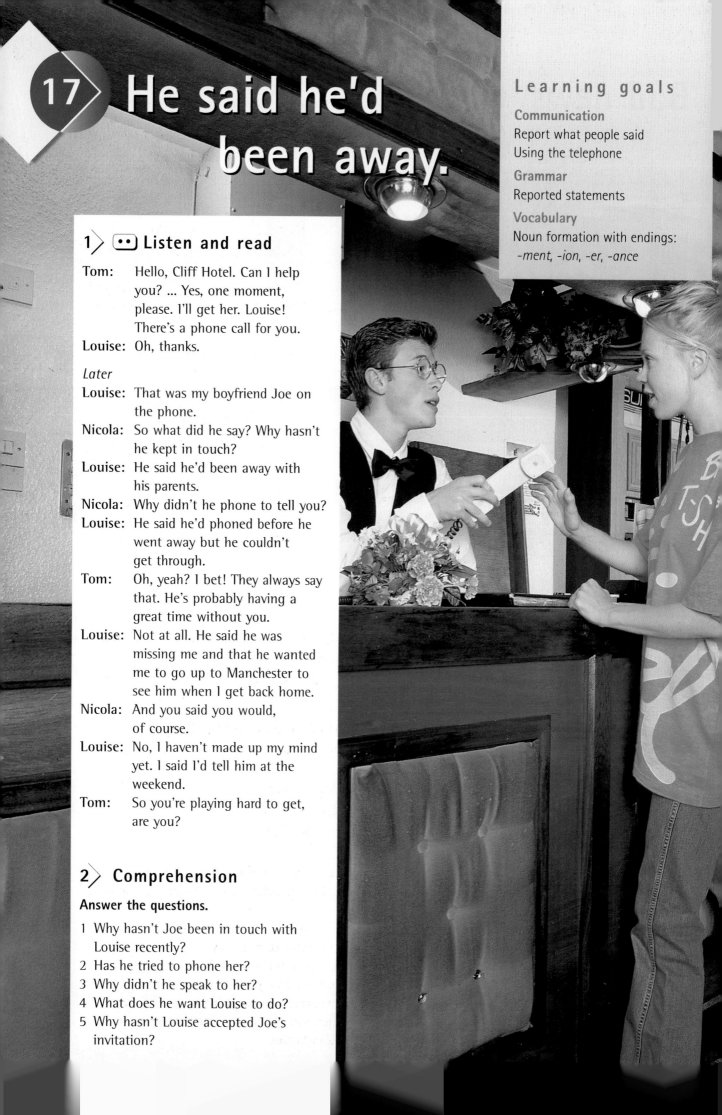

Learning goals

Communication
Report what people said
Using the telephone

Grammar
Reported statements

Vocabulary
Noun formation with endings:
-ment, -ion, -er, -ance

1 ⟩ 👁 Listen and read

Tom: Hello, Cliff Hotel. Can I help you? ... Yes, one moment, please. I'll get her. Louise! There's a phone call for you.

Louise: Oh, thanks.

Later

Louise: That was my boyfriend Joe on the phone.

Nicola: So what did he say? Why hasn't he kept in touch?

Louise: He said he'd been away with his parents.

Nicola: Why didn't he phone to tell you?

Louise: He said he'd phoned before he went away but he couldn't get through.

Tom: Oh, yeah? I bet! They always say that. He's probably having a great time without you.

Louise: Not at all. He said he was missing me and that he wanted me to go up to Manchester to see him when I get back home.

Nicola: And you said you would, of course.

Louise: No, I haven't made up my mind yet. I said I'd tell him at the weekend.

Tom: So you're playing hard to get, are you?

2 ⟩ Comprehension

Answer the questions.

1 Why hasn't Joe been in touch with Louise recently?
2 Has he tried to phone her?
3 Why didn't he speak to her?
4 What does he want Louise to do?
5 Why hasn't Louise accepted Joe's invitation?

Grammar snapshot

Reported statements

Direct speech	Reported speech
'I am Spanish.'	He said (that) he was Spanish.
'We're learning English.'	They said (that) they were learning English.
'I like Tom Cruise.'	She told me (that) she liked Tom Cruise.
'I left at six o'clock.'	He said (that) he had left at six o'clock.
'I've lost my passport.'	She said (that) she had lost her passport.
'We'll phone soon.'	They told her (that) they would phone soon.
'He can't read the board.'	He said (that) he couldn't read the board.

Note

- The word *that* can be omitted, e.g. *She said she didn't like him.*
- *Tell* is always followed by an object pronoun or noun.

Make rules.

Direct speech		Reported speech
1 Present continuous	➤	Past continuous
2 Present simple	➤	...
3 Past simple	➤	...
4 Present perfect	➤	...
5 *will*	➤	...
6 *can*	➤	...

4〉 Practice

a〉 Look back at the dialogue in Exercise 1. Find the reported speech and write Joe and Louise's actual words.

He said he'd been away with his parents.
'I've been away with my parents.'

b〉 Report Louise's part of the conversation with Joe.

Joe: ... and I couldn't get through. Anyway, how are you?
Louise: I'm fine.[1]

> *1 Louise said that she was ...*

Joe: Do you miss me?
Louise: Yes, I'm missing you a lot.[2]

> *2 She said ...*

Joe: I'm missing you, too. Have you met a lot of new people?
Louise: Yes. There's a nice girl called Nicola working at the hotel.[3]
Joe: Oh, is there?
Louise: And I've met a South African guy called Jake.[4]
Joe: I see. So how do you like Newquay?
Louise: I love it. The beaches are fantastic.[5]
Joe: What have you been doing?
Louise: We went to a concert in a beautiful open-air theatre.[6]
Joe: Oh! Listen. When you get back, I want you to come up to see me in Manchester.

3〉 👀 Useful phrases

Listen and repeat.

- [That was Joe] on the phone.
- [Why hasn't he] kept in touch?
- I bet!
- Not at all.
- I haven't made up my mind yet.
- [So you're] playing hard to get, [are you]?

The birth of radio

Today we don't think twice when we turn on the radio, but when a 21-year-old Italian invented it over 100 years ago no one could believe their ears.

One day in 1895 in Bologna, Italy, Guglielmo Marconi sent the world's first radio signal. Using a simple radio transmitter and a receiver, he sent a signal from his attic room to his brother who was hidden in a field a kilometre away. When his brother received the signal he fired a gun. The Italian government showed no interest in young Marconi's invention, but his mother, Annie, who was Irish, believed he had a good idea. So in February of the following year, she sent him to England to meet her cousin who was an important engineer. It was a journey that would change the world.

In England, Marconi and his cousin were joined by two other inventors. In 1897 Marconi formed Marconi's Wireless Telegraph Company in London and started to transmit simple radio signals over long distances. In 1899 he sent the first wireless telegraph across the English

Preparing the kite and aerial to receive Marconi's first transatlantic radio signals

Guglielmo Marconi (1874–1937)
Italian electrical engineer and Nobel prize winner, the inventor of the first radio-signalling system

Channel to France. This meant that ships were now able to send messages from ship to shore if they were in distress.

Marconi had always believed that radio waves could travel round the curve of the earth. By 1901 he had improved his radio system so much that on 12th December he astonished the world by sending the first radio signals across the Atlantic Ocean. They were transmitted from Poldhu in Cornwall, and were received 3,520 kilometres away in St John's, Newfoundland, using an aerial flown in the air by a kite. Marconi's system was soon adopted by the British and Italian navies. From now on, the Marconi company had the monopoly of wireless communication and Marconi became a multi-millionaire.

Marconi is one of the key figures of the twentieth century. He even recognised the military importance of radar and thought of the idea of sending radio signals out into space. When Marconi died in 1937, wireless stations all over the world closed down for two minutes as a mark of respect. Marconi made only one big mistake. He thought that television would never become popular.

5 〉 Read

a〉 Read the text and find words and phrases which mean the same as the following.

1 give something a second thought
2 in danger or difficulty
3 made better
4 amazed
5 total control
6 a person with a lot of money

b〉 Why were the following people and places important in Marconi's life?

1 Bologna was important because it was where Marconi was born and where he ... .

1 Bologna
2 His mother Annie
3 His mother's cousin
4 Poldhu in Cornwall
5 St John's, Newfoundland

c〉 Complete the notes about Marconi and the history of radio communication.

1874	*Marconi was born*
1895	...
1896	...
1897	...
1899	...
1901	...
1937	...

6 〉 Vocabulary helpline

Use word endings to identify parts of speech

You can often guess the part of speech of a word from its ending. For example, words ending in *-ment, -ion, -ance, -ence, -ness* are often nouns.

7 〉 Vocabulary

Noun formation with endings: *-ment, -ion, -er, -ance*

Make words by matching the first part of each word with the correct ending(s).

- -ment
- -ion
- -er
- -ance

1 relation

1 relat-	6 achieve-	11 demonstrat-
2 transmitt-	7 invent-	12 import-
3 receiv-	8 equip-	13 perform-
4 dist-	9 winn-	14 entertain-
5 communicat-	10 govern-	15 educat-

8 〉 Discussion

Do you think radio and telecommunications inventions have improved the quality of our life today or not?

9 〉 Write

Find as much information as you can about an inventor of your choice. Write about him/her using the text about Marconi as a model. Include:

- when and where he/she lived.
- what he/she invented.
- why the achievement was important.
- if it has made people's lives better or worse.

Portable radio 1929   *Modern personal radio/stereo*

10 ⚬⚬ Listen

a> Listen to an extract from a guided tour of the Goonhilly Earth Station in Cornwall. Then complete the notes.

Goonhilly Earth Station

Location: *Lizard peninsula, southern Cornwall, England*
Purpose:
Number of satellite dishes:
Number of satellites:
Historic events: Date
   1
   2

b> Listen again and answer the questions.

1 Why is Goonhilly a good place to build a big satellite dish?
2 How were the first TV signals sent from North America to England?

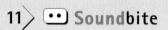

11 ⚬⚬ Sound**bite**

Rising intonation in telephone conversations

⌒   ⌒
Hello? Who's speaking?
(Look at page 123.)

12 Communication

Using the telephone

▶ Hello. Newquay College. Can I help you?
▶ Oh, hello. Can I speak to Sandy Poole, please?
▶ Yes, one moment, please. I'll get her. Sandy! There's a phone call for you.

▶ 865 1479. Lucy Cook speaking.
▶ Hello, Mrs Cook. It's Robert here. Is Nick there?/Could I speak to Nick, please?
▶ I'm not sure. Hold on. I'll find out ... I'm afraid he's out. Can I take a message?
▶ Yes, please. Can you tell him ... ?/ No, it's OK. It doesn't matter. I'll ring back later.
▶ I'll tell him you called.
▶ Thanks.

Make similar telephone conversations for these situations.

1 **Student B:** Turn to page 121.
   Student A: You are in the school secretary's office when the phone rings. You answer it. The secretary is out.

2 **Student B:** Turn to page 121.
   Student A: You are at home. The phone rings. You answer it.

Fast rewind UNITS 16 and 17

Grammar

1> **Complete the conversation with the correct form of** *used to* **and the verbs in brackets.**

A: I (collect) [1] *used to collect* stamps when I was young. (you/collect) [2] ... anything?

B: Nothing, but I (save) [3] ... silver paper.

A: Really? What (you/do) [4] ... with it?

B: We (roll) [5] ... it into big balls and sell them but we (not/make) [6] ... much money.

2> **Complete the sentences with** *so, such* **or** *such a/an.*

He was *so* angry that he put the phone down.

1 They're ... good friends that they never argue.
2 The traffic was ... noisy that they couldn't sleep.
3 We were having ... nice time that we didn't want to go.
4 It was ... interesting programme that we recorded it.
5 They were ... hungry that they ate everything.
6 The project was ... hard work that I need a long rest.
7 The first term at university is ... exciting time that the students never do very much work!

3> **Change the statements into reported speech.**

'I'm a policeman.'
He said (that) he was a policeman.

1 'We're not staying in a hostel.' They said ...
2 'I'm a vegetarian and I don't eat meat.' She said ...
3 'The boys went home at ten o'clock.' They said ...
4 'I've lost my purse.' Nicola said ...
5 'I can't read the writing on the board.' The boy said ...
6 'We'll phone on Saturday.' They said ...
7 'The eggs are delivered fresh every morning.' She said ...
8 'I didn't work the early shift on Sunday.' Tom said ...

4> **Write what the people actually said.**

He said he'd been in London last year.
'I was in London last year.'

1 She said she was having a good time in Ireland.
2 They told us they couldn't get tickets for the concert.
3 He said he'd already eaten a big meal.
4 I said I wouldn't go to the match on Saturday.
5 You told me you swam twenty lengths of the swimming pool every morning.
6 Jake said that he was running the marathon next week.
7 My brother said that he had seen my girlfriend out with someone else.

Vocabulary

5> **Complete the sentences with the correct part of speech from one of the following verbs.**

• sail   • transmit   • entertain   • invent   • smuggle
• bake   • box

We get fresh bread from the *baker* every morning.

1 Frank Sinatra was one of the world's great ... .
2 Is ... a serious crime in your country?
3 They do a lot of ... off the south coast of England.
4 The signals are sent into space from an enormous ... .
5 My brother wants to be a ... but I hate ... as a sport.
6 Who was the ... of the telephone?

Communication

6> **Work in pairs. Student A works in a theatre box office. Student B phones to book some tickets. Put the sentences in the correct order to make the telephone conversation.**

A: *Hello. Box office. How can I help you?*
B: ...

Student A
1 The 28th is fine. The tickets go from £7.50 to £20.
2 Yes, there's a £2 reduction, but we need to see your student cards.
3 Certainly. What would you like to see?
4 Thank you, Mr Hunt. I've reserved four tickets for the 28th.
5 That'll be fine. But you must collect them half an hour before the start. Could I have your name, please?

Student B
a) OK. We'll show them when we collect the tickets.
b) The ballet 'Swan Lake'. We'd like seats for 28th August. How much are the tickets?
c) Hunt, Colin Hunt.
d) Oh, hello. Could I book some seats, please?
e) We'll have four at £7.50. Is it cheaper for students?

18 'The Birds'

Learning goals

Communication
Report what people asked
Ask permission with *Do you mind/Is it all right if I ... ?*

Grammar
Reported questions

Vocabulary
Phrases of approximate time and quantity:
a few (minutes ago), about, a couple of, several, lots of (people), etc.

1 ⚬⚬ Read and listen

a Find words or expressions in the text that mean the same as the following.

1 location of a story
2 far away
3 cut into two or more parts
4 for a short time
5 covered the windows with wood

b Correct the sentences.

1 When Nat saw the black cloud, he knew that it was heavy rain.
2 When Jill's friends got off the bus, Nat wanted them to stay and play for a bit.
3 Nat took Jill home.
4 Nat decided not to stay with the farmer because he didn't have a gun.
5 A small flock of birds first attacked Nat when he was talking to the farmer.
6 Nat was worried because they didn't have any food in the house.

2 Discussion

Why do you think the birds suddenly began to attack humans?
Do you know any other stories or films like this?
How do think this story ends?

3 ⚬⚬ Listen

Listen to how the story ends and make notes. Were you right about the ending?

4 Write

Write the final paragraph of the story. Begin like this:

Nat and his wife prepared themselves for the attack. First they ...

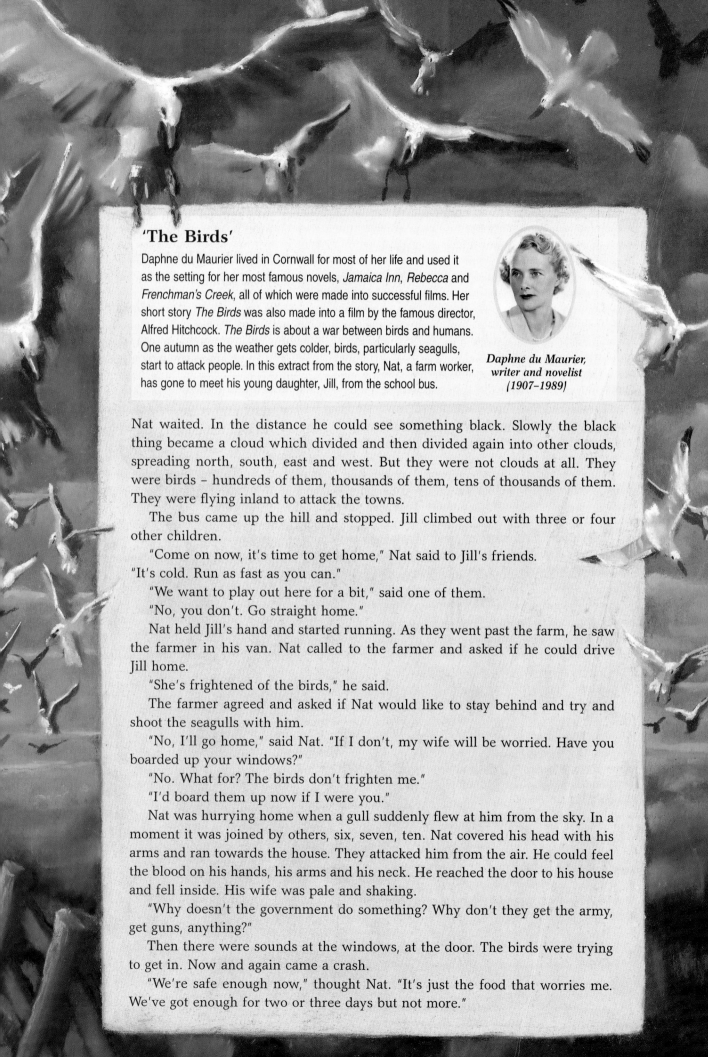

'The Birds'

Daphne du Maurier lived in Cornwall for most of her life and used it as the setting for her most famous novels, *Jamaica Inn*, *Rebecca* and *Frenchman's Creek*, all of which were made into successful films. Her short story *The Birds* was also made into a film by the famous director, Alfred Hitchcock. *The Birds* is about a war between birds and humans. One autumn as the weather gets colder, birds, particularly seagulls, start to attack people. In this extract from the story, Nat, a farm worker, has gone to meet his young daughter, Jill, from the school bus.

Daphne du Maurier, writer and novelist (1907–1989)

Nat waited. In the distance he could see something black. Slowly the black thing became a cloud which divided and then divided again into other clouds, spreading north, south, east and west. But they were not clouds at all. They were birds – hundreds of them, thousands of them, tens of thousands of them. They were flying inland to attack the towns.

The bus came up the hill and stopped. Jill climbed out with three or four other children.

"Come on now, it's time to get home," Nat said to Jill's friends. "It's cold. Run as fast as you can."

"We want to play out here for a bit," said one of them.

"No, you don't. Go straight home."

Nat held Jill's hand and started running. As they went past the farm, he saw the farmer in his van. Nat called to the farmer and asked if he could drive Jill home.

"She's frightened of the birds," he said.

The farmer agreed and asked if Nat would like to stay behind and try and shoot the seagulls with him.

"No, I'll go home," said Nat. "If I don't, my wife will be worried. Have you boarded up your windows?"

"No. What for? The birds don't frighten me."

"I'd board them up now if I were you."

Nat was hurrying home when a gull suddenly flew at him from the sky. In a moment it was joined by others, six, seven, ten. Nat covered his head with his arms and ran towards the house. They attacked him from the air. He could feel the blood on his hands, his arms and his neck. He reached the door to his house and fell inside. His wife was pale and shaking.

"Why doesn't the government do something? Why don't they get the army, get guns, anything?"

Then there were sounds at the windows, at the door. The birds were trying to get in. Now and again came a crash.

"We're safe enough now," thought Nat. "It's just the food that worries me. We've got enough for two or three days but not more."

5 ⟩ 👂 Listen and read

Ken: Do you mind if you have the noise of seagulls in the background, Sue?
Sue: No, Ken. That's fine. OK, Jake. We're ready to start.
Jake: Is it all right if I stand here?
Sue: It looks more natural if you sit.
Jake: Like this?
Sue: That's good.
Jake: Ready when you are.
Sue: Right. Tell us a bit about yourself, Jake.
Jake: OK.

Later

Nicola: You look very pleased with yourself.
Jake: I've just done a TV interview with Sue Turner.
Nicola: What was it about?
Jake: The surf competition – and me of course!
Nicola: Fame at last! What did they ask you?
Jake: They asked me where I was from, how long I'd been surfing – you know – just general stuff.
Nicola: Next stop Hollywood! Have you got your surfboard back, by the way?
Jake: No, worse luck! I'm getting really worried.

6 ⟩ Comprehension

a ⟩ Answer T (true), F (false) or DK (don't know).

1 Sue doesn't mind the sound of the seagulls in the background.
2 Jake looks more relaxed standing up.
3 The interview takes place in the morning.
4 Jake enjoyed doing the interview.
5 Nicola watched the interview later on TV.
6 Jake has found his surfboard.

b ⟩ Talk about it.

Why does Nicola tease Jake?

7 ⟩ 👂 Useful phrases

Listen and repeat.

- Like this? • Ready when you are.
- Tell us a bit about [yourself].
- Fame at last! • Just general stuff.
- Next stop [Hollywood]!
- No, worse luck!

Grammar snapshot

Reported questions

Direct questions	Reported questions		Make rules.
Wh- questions			1 We never use the auxiliaries *do*, *does* or … in reported questions. We use the affirmative form of the verb.
'What's your name?'	She asked him	what his name was.	
'Where do you come from?'		where he came from.	
'When are you leaving?'		when he was leaving.	
Yes/No questions			2 We use the word … to introduce reported *Yes/No* questions.
'Do you like Cornwall?'	She asked him	if he liked Cornwall.	
'Did you go to London first?'		if he had gone to London first.	
'Have you found your surfboard?'		if he had found his surfboard.	
'Can you answer some more questions?'		if he could answer some more questions.	

8 〉 Practice

Complete the items with either the direct or the reported question.

Sue's questions	What Jake reported to Nicola
1 'How old are you?'	…
2 …	She asked if I had got a fan club.
3 'How long have you been surfing?'	…
4 …	She asked me what I thought about Cornwall.
5 'When are you going back home?'	…
6 …	She asked me if I was going to win.
7 'Will you ever come back here?'	…

9 〉 ⦇⦈ Listen

a〉 Listen to an interview with a girl who wants to be a vet. After each of the interviewer's five questions you will hear a *bleep*. Write the questions and briefly note the answers.

1 Why do you want to be a vet? (grew up on a farm/loves animals)

b〉 Now write the questions in reported speech.

1 He asked her why she wanted to be a vet.

10 〉 Over to you

Write down five questions to ask your favourite pop star, sports star, TV or film star. Imagine that you interviewed the star. Tell the rest of the class the questions you asked and the answers which the star gave.

I asked Vialli which team he had played for first. He said he had played for Juventus. Then I asked him if he was married.

11 › Vocabulary

Phrases of approximate time and quantity

Time	
about (two) a couple of a few several	minutes/hours/days/ weeks/months/years (ago)
(not) for some time (not) for ages	

Quantity	
about (three) a couple of a few several lots of hundreds/thousands of loads of	people

Ask and answer in pairs.

1 A: *When did you last go to the hairdresser's?*
  B: *I haven't been to the hairdresser's for ages.*

1 When did you last go to the hairdresser's?
2 When did you last have a Maths exam?
3 When did you last go to the cinema?
4 How many people are there at your school?
5 How many times have you been late for school this year?
6 How many CDs and cassettes have you got?

12 › Speaking helpline

Express mood through intonation

When learning English, it is important to listen to *how* people say things as well as what they say. A native speaker uses intonation (his/her voice goes up and down) to indicate mood and attitude. For example, this can make a difference between sounding polite or impolite.

13 › 👀 Soundbite

Rising intonation to ask polite questions

Do you mind if I sit here?
(Look at page 123.)

14 › Communication

Asking permission

▶ Is it all right if I sit here?
▶ Yes, sure./Yes, of course./I'm sorry, I'm afraid (it's taken.)

▶ Do you mind if I ask you a few questions?
▶ No, not at all./No, go ahead./No, that's OK.
   Well, actually (I'm a bit busy at the moment.)

Make similar conversations for these situations. Imagine you are staying with a host family while you are on an English language course in Britain or the USA. Continue each conversation if you can.

1 You come home after class and would like to make yourself a cup of hot chocolate. Your host is quite happy about that and tells you where everything is in the kitchen. Thank him/her and ask if he/she has had a good day.

2 You want to watch a sports programme on TV. Unfortunately your host wants to watch the news which is on at the same time.

Nicola to the rescue

Read the story and try to guess the missing words. Then listen and see if you were right.

1

I'm off now, Morris.

Yes, OK. By the way, Tom left his watch in the kitchen.

I'll take it to his house. I asked him if he _____ and he said he was.

2

I'll see you later. _____ walk round _____ .

_____ ? I'd like some fresh air.

No, not at all.

3

Can you see who I can see! It's _____ .

And isn't that _____ ?

You're right. Quick. Let's _____ .

4

Into the car, you two. You've both got a few questions to answer.

Why? _____ near the surf club!

5

_____ ?

No, go ahead. It's switched on.

Hi, Jake! It's Nicola. Guess what! _____ !

6

7

Great! I never thought I _____ . Thanks, Nicola, you're a star!

POLICE P754 OPP

19 He's too good to fall.

Learning goals

Communication
Say the right thing

Grammar
too + adjective / adverb + *to*
(not) + adjective / adverb +
enough to
Verb + infinitive / gerund

Vocabulary
Neutral and strong adjectives

1> **Listen and read**

It's the day of the surf championship finals.

Nicola: How are you feeling?
Jake: Brilliant!
Nicola: Who's your main rival?
Jake: Paddy Stone. He's pretty good but ...
Nicola: But what?
Jake: He's not good enough to win!
PA: *Attention, please! The Surf Final is about to start.*

The competition is in progress

Nicola: Look at that enormous wave!
Tom: Yeah, that *is* big. It's going to be too powerful for him. He'll fall!
Nicola: No, he's too good to fall.
Tom: Famous last words!
Nicola: Oh, no! It's a wipeout! Poor Jake!

Later

PA: *And the winner is ... Paddy Stone from New Zealand!*
Nicola: Bad luck, Jake!
Jake: That was terrible!
Nicola: Surely you don't mind losing sometimes!
Tom: That's right. Win some, lose some!
Jake: I really wanted that prize money.
Nicola: Money isn't everything, you know.
Jake: It is to me.
Nicola: Obviously. Coming, Tom?

2 Comprehension

Answer T (true), F (false) or
DK (don't know).

1 Jake is not feeling very confident.
2 Paddy Stone is one of the
   favourites to win.
3 Jake is knocked off his board.
4 Jake doesn't mind losing.
5 Nicola is upset by Jake's attitude.

3 💬 Useful phrases

Listen and repeat.

- Famous last words! • Poor [Jake]!
- Win some, lose some!
- Money isn't everything.
- Obviously. • Coming, [Tom]?

Grammar flash

too + **adjective/adverb** + *to*
He's **too** good **to** fall.
He ran **too** slowly **to** win.

(not) + **adjective/adverb** + *enough to*
He's **(not)** good **enough to** win.
He does**n't** train hard **enough to** win.

Make rules by choosing *before* **or** *after*.
1 *Too* usually comes before/after an adjective or adverb.
2 *Enough* usually comes before/after an adjective or adverb.

4 💬 Soundbite   Sentence stress

He's <u>too</u> good to <u>fall</u>.
He's <u>not good</u> enough to <u>win</u>. (Look at page 123.)

5 Practice

Use an adjective or adverb with *too/enough* **together
with a verb to complete the sentences.**

Adjective/Adverb
- old • big • cold • tired • hard • fast • hot

Verb
- cook • do • get • put • notice • go out • go

1 His surfboard is too big to put in the back of the car.

1 His surfboard is ... in the back of the car.
2 He was driving ... the scenery.
3 I'm going to bed. I'm ... my homework.
4 My little sister isn't ... on her own.
5 It's ... swimming today.
6 The barbecue isn't ... the chicken yet.
7 He doesn't work ... good marks in his exams.

6 Over to you

Discuss the questions in pairs.

1 How brave are you?   2 How fit are you?
  Would you try: Are you able to:
  - scuba diving?   • run 1,000 metres?
  - hang gliding?   • run up four flights of stairs?
  - bungee jumping?   • cycle ten kilometres?

A: *I'm not brave enough to try scuba diving. What about you?*
B: *Yes, I think I am. But I'm not brave enough to try bungee
   jumping.*
A: *Nor am I.*

A superstar *with attitude*

Will Smith tells Barry Lister about his attitude to life

● How important is it for you to make a success of things?

It's very important. I've always wanted to make something of my life and I guess I've been pretty lucky. The American TV comedy series *Fresh Prince of Bel Air*, which started in 1991, and the films *Independence Day* in 1996 and *Men in Black* in 1997 were major turning points in my career.

● How do you relax?

I enjoy playing basketball and I love swimming and bowling. But I also spend hours playing video games! My other real love is music. I love all sorts, particularly soul, R and B and rap. In fact I started my career as a rapper at the age of fourteen. I played with a friend in clubs in Philadelphia. We had a big hit in 1986 with "Parents just don't understand". Good title, huh?

● What sort of things make you laugh?

Silly things make me laugh. On the set of *Men in Black*, Tommy Lee Jones and I often had shoe-kicking contests. A favourite game was to put up a trash can twenty metres away, take off our shoes and practise kicking them into the can. Brilliant fun!

● Does money mean a lot to you?

Yes, it does, but not as much now as it used to. I made a fortune early on from the TV series and I went wild. I bought several Cadillacs, flew in a private jet and moved into an enormous house I didn't really like. But then I lost nearly all of it through some bad business deals. Now I look after my money quite carefully. I have a lovely house, a car and five dogs but nothing else really expensive.

● If you had one fantasy wish in life, what would it be?

I'd like to be able to fly, like Superman!

● What sort of things annoy you?

I sometimes get annoyed when I have to wait around on the film set. And I hate waiting for trains and planes and people.

● What are your best and worst qualities?

In work I have lots of energy and I'm a perfectionist. I like the idea of a job well-done. But at home I'm too lazy and untidy to win any medals! My clothes are always lying around and I hate doing the washing-up!

● What important lesson have you learnt so far in life?

I've learnt that money is not the most important thing in life.

Before you read

Which films has Will Smith starred in?
Have you seen any of them?
Do you like him?

7> Read

a> Read the interview with Will Smith and complete the information.

Name:	Will Smith
Date/Place of birth:	1968 Philadelphia, USA
Career so far:	
1982–1986:	
1991:	
1996:	
1997:	
Fantasy wish:	
Good qualities:	
Bad qualities:	

b> Read the interview again and find words or phrases which mean the same as the following.

1 wastepaper bin
2 a lot of money
3 very big
4 imaginary
5 irritate

Verb + infinitive/gerund

Infinitive with *to*
He wanted **to win**.
I decided **to do** the film.

Gerund (*-ing* form)
I enjoy **playing** basketball.
I hate **waiting** for trains.

Which of the verbs below are followed by an infinitive with *to* and which by an *-ing* form?
• decide • want • mind
• promise • enjoy • hope
• offer • miss • agree • finish
• seem • give up • avoid
• manage • refuse • practise
• expect • hate

8> Practice

a> Complete these sentences so that they are true and discuss them.

1 I have decided ... next year.
2 When I get home from school, I usually want ...
3 When I'm on holiday I don't mind ...
4 I never trust people who promise ...
5 At weekends I enjoy ...
6 When I leave school, I hope ...
7 I have friends who never offer ...

b> Make sentences using the remaining verbs from the Grammar flash.

9> Over to you

Ask your partner the questions in the Will Smith interview. Then tell the class about some interesting answers your partner gave.

10 > Vocabulary

Neutral and strong adjectives

- big • terrified • small • starving
- good • enormous • exhausted
- bad • brilliant • tired • terrible
- afraid • hungry • tiny

Make pairs of neutral and strong adjectives from the list above.

Neutral	Strong
big	*enormous*

11 > Practice

Practise the conversation using a different pair of adjectives each time.

A: *Was his house big?*
B: *Big? It was enormous!*

1 Was his house big?
2 Your bedroom is quite small, isn't it?
3 Are you feeling tired?
4 I think he's afraid of the dark.
5 Are you hungry?
6 You've had a bad day, haven't you?
7 She's a good singer, isn't she?

12 > Communication

Saying the right thing

1 Have a good trip.
2 I hope you pass your driving test.
3 Give my regards to your parents.
4 Have a nice time.
5 Don't do too much work!
6 Send me a postcard.
7 Take care!
8 Good luck!
9 Don't do anything I wouldn't do!

Match an expression from the list above with one or more of these replies.

a) Yes, so do I.
b) Thanks. Same to you.
c) Yes, I will.
d) Don't worry, I won't!
e) Thanks!
f) Thanks, I'm sure I will.

1 Have a good trip! - b), c), e), f)

13 > 👄 Listen

a > **Listen to three 'goodbye' scenes and say where the people are.**

b > **In pairs, make up a 'goodbye' scene for two people in the picture below. With another pair, roleplay your scenes to each other.**

14 > Revision helpline

Keep up your English

1 Look through the book again and make a note of any units you found particularly difficult. Perhaps some of the grammar was hard, or maybe there was a difficult area of vocabulary.
2 Look again at the Grammar Builder section in your Language Booster and the Unit-by-unit word list in this Students' Book so that you can revise areas where you have problems. Ask your teacher's advice if you need it.
3 Try to use your English whenever you can!

Grammar

1 Change the direct questions into reported questions.

'What's your name?' She asked me ...
She asked me what my name was.

'Did you see the film on TV last night?' He wanted to know ...
He wanted to know if I had seen the film on TV last night.

1 'Where do you come from?' They asked us ...
2 'When are you both leaving?' He wanted to know ...
3 'Do you like Cornwall?' The reporter asked Jake ...
4 'Did you go to London first?' She asked me ...
5 'How old are you?' The reporter asked me ...
6 'Can you teach me to surf?' Nicola asked him ...
7 'Will you ever visit Cornwall again?' She asked Jake ...
8 'What are you going to do when you get home?' He asked us ...

2 Complete the sentences using the cues in brackets with *too* or *enough*.

It's sometimes (hot/eat a lot)
It's sometimes too hot to eat a lot.

My sister isn't (old/go to school alone)
My sister isn't old enough to go to school alone.

1 The water isn't (hot/to make the tea).
2 The weather (cold/go to the beach).
3 He says he not (brave/try surfing).
4 My school bag is (light/carry on the back of my bike).
5 He doesn't work (hard/get top marks in his exam).
6 My room is (small/work in comfortably).
7 I'm (not fit/swim 1000 metres).
8 They want to go to bed. They're (tired/watch TV).

Vocabulary

3 Choose the correct expression of time or quantity to complete each sentence.

They arrived in Newquay ... . (four weeks ago/for ages)
They arrived in Newquay four weeks ago.

1 The stadium was packed with ... football fans. (some/hundreds of)
2 I haven't been to the cinema ... . (for ages/for long)
3 We've got ... cokes in the fridge. (many/plenty of)
4 A: Have you got loads of CDs?
   B: No, I've only got ... . (several/a few)
5 The last time I went to the dentist was exactly ... . (last year/a year ago)
6 ... people were taken ill after the meal. (Several/Few)

4 Complete each sentence using one of these verbs in the infinitive or the gerund (*-ing* form).

• tell • lose • do • play • tidy • win • let • visit

Jake really wanted *to win* the surf championships.

1 Do children still enjoy ... jigsaw puzzles?
2 Our teacher has agreed ... us have a class party.
3 Some people waste hours ... video games.
4 I promise not ... anyone about your sister.
5 We're hoping ... San Francisco next summer.
6 Jake didn't expect ... the surf championship.
7 Have you finished ... your bedroom?

Communication

5 Work in pairs. Roleplay an interview with a new American pop star who is visiting your country. Start with Student A as the interviewer and Student B as the pop star. Then change roles.

Student A
• Get permission to ask a few personal questions.
• Check his/her nationality.
• Find out about his/her journey to your capital city.
• Ask if he/she has been to your country before.
• Find out which cities he/she is going to perform in and on which dates.
• Find out what his/her next single will be.
• Wish him/her good luck and say goodbye.

Student B
• You have just arrived in the capital city. You travelled by car from the airport.
• It's the first time you have been in A's country.
• You are performing tomorrow in the capital and in a different city each day next week (give places and dates).
• Your next single is called after your best friend.

Progress update Units 18 and 19

How do you rate your progress? Tick the chart.

	Excellent ★★★★	Good ★★★	OK ★★	Can do better ★
Grammar				
Vocabulary				
Communication				

After three days dolphins help boy break lifelong silence

The boy who was taught to talk by dolphins

by our Health Correspondent

For young Nikki Brice, the daily swimming sessions with the dolphins in a pool in Florida, USA, were simply part of a fun holiday with his family. But the real purpose was to see if swimming with dolphins could motivate him to talk.

When Nikki was born, he was starved of oxygen. All his life he had never spoken a word, even though he had the physical ability to speak. All the techniques which were tried in Britain had failed, so eventually, in desperation, Tabitha, his mother, took him to the dolphin pool in Florida to try to get him to talk.

Tabitha Brice, from Weston-super-Mare in Somerset, flew to Florida with Nikki after raising £10,500 with the help of family, friends and celebrities. Nikki was given a combination of conventional speech therapy and daily forty-minute swimming sessions in a pool with a team of eight dolphins. After just three days of the seventeen-day treatment at the Dolphin Human Therapy Centre in Miami, Nikki spoke his first magic word.

It was one marvellous morning that the breakthrough came. Nikki's mother was taking him out of the pool when he firmly grabbed her hand, pointed to the dolphins in the pool and said: 'In.'

'He was telling us that he wanted to get back in the water,' said Mrs Brice. 'We just stood there in shock because it was so unexpected.' Since that first word, Nikki has gone from strength to strength, and has spoken other words like 'please' and 'duck'.

Doctors at the Miami centre say they are very pleased that Nikki has spoken so soon after starting his treatment. A speech therapist in London said that this kind of treatment would not repair any brain damage but if a child was suffering from lack of confidence, swimming with dolphins might help.

Before Nikki's breakthrough, Mrs Brice said that they had only heard about, but not seen, children getting better. 'I had never expected Nikki to make such good progress so quickly but now we are seeing it before our eyes. I'm hoping that his next words will be "Hello Mum"! There is something magical that happens between children and dolphins, something I don't think we will ever fully understand.'

Before you read

Do you know of any stories of dolphins helping humans?

1〉 Read

a〉 Read the text and find words or phrases which mean the same as the following.

1 encourage
2 deprived of
3 methods
4 in despair
5 famous people
6 normal or usual
7 sudden good result
8 seized
9 surprising
10 mend

b〉 Answer the questions.

1 What was wrong with Nikki?
2 What had happened to him earlier in life?
3 Why did his parents decide to take him to Miami?
4 How did they raise the money for it?
5 How do medical experts explain the success of the treatment?

2〉 Speak

Interview the Brice family in Miami. One of you is a reporter and the other is Mrs Brice.

A: *Can you tell us about Nikki?*
B: *He can't speak. He hasn't been able to speak since ...*
A: *What happened?*
B: *...*
A: *Why have you come to ... ?*

Nikki with his mother, Tabitha

3〉 ⏺ Listen

Listen to a speech therapist who specialises in treating people who stammer. Then answer the questions.

1 How does she help children overcome a stammer?
2 How common is the problem?
3 Name some well-known people who stammer.
4 What is a possible cause?
5 How successful is the treatment?
6 What example does she give of a link between bullying and stammering?

4〉 Discussion

How would you help someone with a stammer?

5〉 Write

Write a formal letter to the Director of the Miami Therapy Centre asking if it is possible to work as an assistant in the dolphin pool during your holidays.

• Give a few details about yourself and your education.
• Describe your level of English.
• Say the dates you would like to come.
• Ask for further information about the centre.
• Close your letter.

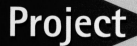

Project ④ Snapshot of inventions

A ▶ **A twentieth-century invention**

Choose one of the items below (or one of your own) and write a project about it to show how it has improved the quality of people's lives today.

- a personal stereo
- a mobile phone
- a calculator
- a refrigerator
- a microwave
- a TV and video
- a washing machine
- a tumble drier
- a fridge-freezer
- a hi-fi system
- a computer

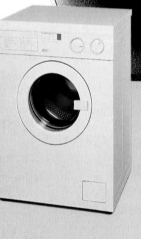

Describe it and say when it was invented.

<u>A personal stereo</u>
A personal stereo is a small, portable machine for playing tapes, which are listened to through headphones. Some personal stereos have special features like an auto-reverse system and an anti-roll mechanism to make the tape run smoothly and play good quality stereophonic sound. The first personal stereo, the Sony Walkman, was introduced in

Say why you think it has improved the quality of life.

It has improved the quality of life because you can listen to your favourite music wherever you are – in the street, in the park, even on a bus or train. You can also listen to music while you are doing sports. The most important thing is that you do not disturb other people with

---

B ▶ **An invention that has improved someone's life**

Interview two older members of your family. Ask which inventions of the twentieth century they think have improved the quality of their lives and why. Then report the interviews.

<u>Interview 1</u>
<u>Name:</u>   Louisa Sutton
<u>Relation:</u> My grandmother
<u>Invention:</u> The washing machine and tumble drier

When I asked my grandmother which invention had improved the quality of her life she said it was the washing machine and tumble drier. She told me that her mother used to do all the family washing by hand but when my grandmother got married she got a washing machine as a present. She said it was wonderful because

Real feelings

Nicola! I thought _____ !

You know I wouldn't _____ .

Have a good trip back. _____ .

No, I won't. Take care.

The time has gone so quickly.

Yes, it has. _____ to your Mum.

_____ .

These are for you. I'm _____ you.

_____ you too!

By the way, I'm coming back here next holidays!

_____ !

Good luck with college next term. I'll phone! Bye!

How funny! I always _____ Louise.

I will survive is one of the great disco dancing songs of the 1970s. It was recorded by Gloria Gaynor, a black singer with a powerful voice and has become a disco classic.

I will survive

At first I was afraid, I was petrified.
Kept thinking I could never [1]............ without you by my side.
But then I spent so [2]............ thinking how you did me wrong,
And I grew [3]............ , and I learned how to get along.
And so you're back! From outer space!
I just walked in to find you here
with that sad look upon your [4]............ .
I should have changed that stupid lock,
I should have made you leave your [5]............ .
If I'd have known for just one second,
[6]............ be back to bother me.

Chorus

Go on! Now go! Walk out the door.
Just turn around now, 'cause you're not welcome any more.
Weren't you the one who tried to [7]............ me with goodbye?
Did you think I'd crumble?
Did you think I'd lay down and die?
Oh, no. Not I! I will survive.
Oh, as long as I know how to love, I know [8]............ .
I've got all my life to live. I've got all my love [9]............ .
And I'll survive. I will survive. Hey! Hey!

It took all the strength I had not to fall apart.
Kept trying hard to mend the pieces of my broken heart.
And I spent oh, so many nights just feeling sorry for [10]............ .
I used to [11]............ , but now I hold my head up high.
And you see me, [12]............ .
I'm not that chained up little person still in love with you.
And so you felt like dropping in, and just expect me to be [13]............ ,
But now I'm saving all my loving for [14]............ who's loving me.

Repeat chorus

1> 👀 Read the lyrics of the song and guess which of these words and phrases fits each gap. Then listen and see if you were right.

• face • key • free • cry • myself • hurt
• strong • I'll stay alive • many nights • you'd
• somebody new • someone • live • to give

2> Find words in the song which mean the same as the following.

1 very frightened   2 treated someone badly
3 unhappy   4 to break into pieces   5 to repair
6 visiting someone unexpectedly

3> List any other disco classics you know.
Find out the most popular song in your class.

Student B section

Unit 1 8⟩ Interaction

Student B: Read about Ryan and answer Student A's questions. Then ask Student A questions and complete the chart about Michelle.

Snapshot of part-time jobs

Ryan Carter lives in London with his parents and his brother.

❝I'm helping my uncle on a market stall. I sell posters, cassettes and CDs. At the moment everyone is buying Britpop. The money is quite good. I only work on Saturday and I get £20 for the day. Part-time jobs are often very boring but I enjoy this job very much. I'm really interested in music. In my spare time I play in a band and I read a lot about the pop scene so I can help people to choose what they want. That's the bit I like best about the job.❞

A: *Where does Ryan come from?*
B: *He comes from ... .*
A: *What part-time job is he doing at the moment?*
   What sort of things does he do in his job?
   When does he work?
   How much does he earn?
   What does he like about the job?
   What does he do in his free time?

Michelle
Home town/city:
Part-time job:
Duties:
Work days:
Pay:
Best part of job:
Other interests:

Unit 9 15⟩ Interaction

Student B: It is 5 p.m. on 1st October 1996. You are Kate Winslet and you are making the film *Titanic*. Use the information below to answer Student A's questions.

Kate Winslet
'I was made up at 10 a.m.'
'I went into the water at 2 p.m.'
'I started work on *Titanic* on 1st September 1996.'
'I made my first film in New Zealand in 1994.'

Change parts. You are in Mexico watching the filming of *Titanic*. Student A is Leonardo DiCaprio. Use the cues below to ask Student A questions with *How long?*

B: *How long have you been wearing make-up today, Leonardo?*
A: *Since seven o'clock this morning.*
B: *Oh, so you've been wearing make-up for ten hours?*

Leonardo DiCaprio
1 wear make-up today?
2 stand in the water?
3 make this film?
4 act in films?

Unit 12 7⟩ Interaction

Student B: Look at the chart about different crops and their food products and answer Student A's questions. Then ask Student A questions to complete your chart. Try to add some information of your own about each crop.

A: *Where are olives grown?*
B: *Olives are grown in countries like Spain, Italy, Greece and Turkey.*
A: *What are they used for?*
B: *They're used to make olive oil, which is exported all over the world. They're also used as a basic food.*

Crop	Country	Product
1 olives	e.g. Spain, Italy, Greece, Turkey	olive oil, basic food
2 grapes	... ...	
3 oranges	e.g. Spain, the USA	orange juice, marmalade
4 wheat	... ...	
5 rice	e.g. India, China, Japan	basic food, breakfast cereal

Unit 16 11⟩ Communication

1 Student B: You are in London and want to visit a special exhibition at the Tate Gallery. You want to know if there are special rates for students. You have your student card with you.

2 Student B: You work at the theatre box office. The cheapest seats for *West Side Story* are £15. There are no special rates for students.

Unit 17 12⟩ Communication

1 Student B: You are at home from school because you are ill. You phone the school to tell the school secretary.

2 Student B: You phone Student A's brother to arrange to meet him at the cinema at 7 p.m. Student A answers.

Answer key

Take a break songs

California Girls
1 they wear   2 southern   3 farmers'   4 feel all right
5 at night   6 coast   7 the girls   8 in the sand
9 this great big world   10 I've seen   11 to get back
12 in the world

I just called to say 'I love you'
1 The correct order is: 1i); 2d); 3j); 4g); 5l); 6k); 7f);
   8c); 9b); 10a); 11m); 12e); 3h)
2 Category 1: 1 New Year's Day   2 Saturday
                   3 Halloween   4 Christmas
   Category 2: 1 April   2 June   3 July   4 August
   Category 3: 1 spring   2 summer   3 autumn

When I'm sixty-four
1 losing my hair   2 quarter to three   3 You'll be older
4 go for a ride   5 who could ask for more?
6 rent a cottage   7 on your knee   8 Send me a postcard
9 mean to say   10 fill in a form

I will survive
1 live   2 many nights   3 strong   4 face   5 key
6 you'd   7 hurt   8 I'll stay alive   9 to give   10 myself
11 cry   12 somebody new   13 free   14 someone

Soundbite exercises

Unit 1 5 ⟩ (••) Soundbite

Weak form / ə / in two-syllable words
singer sailor

Listen and repeat.

/ ə / singer sailor teacher drummer swimmer
       diver waiter
a diver and a surfer
She's a singer and a dancer.
He's a teacher at a high school and a waiter at night.

Unit 2 7 ⟩ (••) Soundbite

Elision: the sound / dʒ / as in / ˈdɪdʒʊ /
Did you like it?

Listen and repeat.

/ dʒ / Did you like it?
        Did you hear it?
        What did you think of it?
        Did you see her?
        What did you say to her?

Unit 3 8 ⟩ (••) Soundbite

Falling intonation on *Wh-* questions

What are you doing on Saturday?

a) Listen and repeat.

on Saturday?   doing on Saturday?

What are you doing on Saturday?

to wear? going to wear? What are you going to wear?
know? will you know? When will you know?

b) Now listen and repeat the complete sentences again.

What are you doing on Saturday?
What are you going to wear?
When will you know?

Unit 4 3 ⟩ (••) Soundbite

Word stress in adjectives
popular unpopular

Listen and repeat.

popular – unpopular   possible – impossible
practical – impractical   interesting – uninteresting
fashionable – unfashionable

Unit 6 4 ⟩ (••) Soundbite

The sound / ɪŋ / working waiting having

a) Listen and repeat.

/ ɪŋ / working waiting having
        He was working at night.
        They were waiting inside.
        I'm having a good time.

b) Now listen and repeat the sentences.
We were walking and running around.
He was having a holiday in Canada.

Unit 7 5 ⟩ (••) Soundbite

Falling intonation with question tags
Question tags have a falling intonation when the speaker is
fairly sure of the answer and just wants to check information.

You're Nicola, aren't you?

a) Listen and repeat.

You're Nicola, aren't you?

Question tags also have a falling intonation when the speaker
is making a remark.

It's cold, isn't it?

b) Listen and repeat.

It's cold, isn't it?

c) Now listen and repeat the sentences.

1 She speaks English, doesn't she?
2 You don't live here, do you?
3 It's hot today, isn't it?
4 They aren't happy here, are they?
5 The hotel wasn't very big, was it?
6 You didn't see Morris, did you?

Unit 8 6 ⟩ (••) Soundbite

Elision between two consonants
baked potatoes fried bread

a) Listen and repeat.

baked potatoes fried bread boiled potatoes fried potatoes
mashed potatoes burnt toast burnt sausages

b) Now listen and repeat the sentences.

Some boiled potatoes and some baked potatoes.
I prefer mashed potatoes to fried potatoes.
Do you want fried bread with your grilled sausages?
I don't mind burnt toast but I don't like burnt sausages.

Unit 9 12 ⟩ (••) Soundbite

Weak form / bɪn /
Have you **been** waiting long?

Listen and repeat the sentences.

Have you been waiting long?
Yes, I've been waiting for ages.
He's been waiting since ten o'clock.
She's been learning English for three years.
They've been travelling in Mexico for weeks.
How long have your cousins been staying?
She's been playing lead guitar in the band for a year.

Unit 11   4⟩ 😊 Sound bite

The sound / l / in initial, medial and final position
Let's   Nicola   I'll

a) Listen and repeat.

/ l /   Let's   Nicola   I'll

b) Now listen and repeat the sentences.

I'll call Nicola and let her know.
They live in Poland.
Say hello to Luke and Jill.
He'll come if you like.
Larry and Bill will be late as well.

Unit 12   10⟩ 😊 Sound bite

Syllable deletion
interested   difference

Listen and repeat.

interested	He's interested in History.
interesting	He's a very interesting man.
difference	What's the difference?
different	You've got a different hairstyle.
secretary	He's First Secretary at the Embassy.
comfortable	The armchair was very comfortable.

Unit 13   13⟩ 😊 Sound bite

Intonation of conditionals
If I were you, I wouldn't do anything.

Listen and repeat.

I wouldn't do anything.   If I were you, I wouldn't do anything.
I'd phone him.   If I were you, I'd phone him.
I wouldn't go.   If I were you, I wouldn't go.
I'd tell him to go away.   If I were you, I'd tell him to go away.

Unit 14   11⟩ 😊 Sound bite

Sentence stress
He told us to stop.

Listen and repeat.

He told us to stop.
He asked him to leave.
She asked me to wait.

He told her to hurry.
He asked her to tell him.
We asked them to buy one.

They wanted me to go.
She wanted us to sing.
We wanted her to stay.

Unit 16   13⟩ 😊 Sound bite

Emphatic stress with *so* and *such*
so tired   such a cold day

Listen and repeat.

so tired   I'm so tired.
so nice   She's so nice.
so famous   He's so famous.
so interesting   It's so interesting.

such a cold day   It's such a cold day.
such a great film   It's such a great film.
such an expensive shop   It's such an expensive shop.
such an important day   It's such an important day.

Unit 17   11⟩ 😊 Sound bite

Rising intonation in telephone conversations
Hello? Who's speaking?

Listen and repeat.

Hello? Who's speaking?
Who's that? Yes? Really?
Who shall I say it is?
Who do you want to speak to?
Can I take a message?
Could you take a message?
Could you see if she's in?

Unit 18   13⟩ 😊 Sound bite

Rising intonation to ask polite questions
Do you mind if I sit here?

Listen and repeat.

sit here   if I sit here   Do you mind if I sit here?
stand   if I stand   Is it all right if I stand?
some questions   if I ask some questions   Do you mind if I ask some questions?
beach   to the beach   Could you tell me the way to the beach?

Unit 19   4⟩ 😊 Sound bite

Sentence stress
He's too good to fall.
He's not good enough to win.

Listen and repeat.

He's too good to fall.
I'm too tired to sleep.
It's too cold to swim.
She's too angry to talk.

He's not good enough to win.
It's not hot enough to swim.
She's not clever enough to pass.
It's not safe enough to drive.
It's not cool enough to eat.

Vocabulary and expressions

Unit 1

Jobs and occupations

Nouns ending in er, -r, -or
builder
drummer
reporter
runner
singer
surfer
diver
driver
manager
actor
sailor
conductor

career
certificate
championships
choir
compete
crab
crowded
electronics
improve
invitation
least (at ...)
lifeguard
lovely (How ...)
part-time
qualifications
seaside resort
shifts (to work ...)
South Africa
surfing
tan (n.)
technical college
unload
waitress
water sports

Unit 2

Past time adverbials
at midday
in 1998
last week
on Friday
this morning
two hours ago
yesterday morning

Means of transport
ages (for ...)
almost
altogether

annoy
artificial
bunk
climber
clumsy
compartment
delay (n.)
disabled
drag
easy (take things ...)
expedition
fact (in ...)
faithfully (yours ...)
foot (of a
   mountain)
forward (look ... to)
hard (adv.)
impossible
inspire
keep going
mountaineer
nightmare
signal failure
snow-covered
so (conj.)
step on
take (time)
transport (n.)
trip over
wake someone up

Unit 3

The natural environment
bay
beach
cave
cliff(s)
coast/coastline
cove
field
forest
hill
island
lake
moor
mountain
river
rock
sea
tree
valley

amusements
attract
branch (of an
   organisation)
castle
coastal
combine
connected
   (be ... with)

disappear
enthusiast
fancy (Do you ...
   going?)
frequently
fudge
get away from
gymnast
include
industry
inland
inventor
isolated
legend
level (n.)
literature
mainland
major
mild
mining
odd (= strange)
offer (v.)
paradise
plenty
ruined
sanctuary
sculptor
seal
seaside
Silly me!
spectacular
surprisingly
telecommunications
tourism
unemployment
wireless signal

Unit 4

Adjectives with negative prefixes
im-, in-, un-
(im)mature
(im)possible
(im)practical
(in)correct
(in)dependent
(in)formal
(un)comfortable
(un)fashionable
(un)happy
(un)healthy
(un)important
(un)interesting
(un)pleasant
(un)popular
(un)successful
(un)usual

absolutely
addict
barman

behave
board (= surfboard)
cold (n.)
combination
confidence
control (n.)
economy
essential
gorilla
leash
leave (time free)
lifestyle
much (stronger)
off (time ...)
originate
polluted
powerful
radical
since
so-called
spread
sunglasses
suntan
surf (n.)
surfboard
timing
ugly
useful
wave (in the sea)
wetsuit
wipeout (n.)

Unit 5
administrative
allow
apartheid
Asian
bench
buffalo
campaign
democracy
democratic
dense
descent
development
diamond
dramatic
elected
exist
found (v.)
game reserve
government
hold elections
huge
hunter
inhumane
judicial
landscape
legislative
leopard
marriage
mineral

official (adj.)
opinion (in my ...) ·
penguin
principle
prison
public transport
racism
racist
system
textiles
varied
whale-watching

Unit 6

Verbs of movement
bounce
dive
fall
jump
leap
sink
swim

Prepositions of motion
across
along
down
from
into
past
over
through
towards
under
up

accidentally
arrest (v.)
breathe
closed-circuit TV
clue
edge
engine
experienced
father-in-law
footpath
fortunately
free (v.)
gear (in ...)
hole
incident
jetty
jump leads
lead (v.)
manage
marina
mistake (by ...)
motorist
mound
mouth-to-mouth

pancake
pasty (Cornish ...)
pick up
repairer
resuscitation
scuba diver
security guard
steering wheel
take off (glasses)
tank
tide
worry (n.)
yachtsman

Unit 7

Clothes and parts of clothes
collar
cuffs
hem
laces
pockets
sleeves
turn-ups

Humour
cartoon
joke
satire
sense of humour
situation comedy
   (sit-com)
slapstick
stand-up comedy/
   comedian

care
change (clothes)
culture
deputy
disaster
fan mail
fussy
individual
innocent
iron (v.)
largely
millionaire
naturally
necessarily
New Year's Day
selfish
shared
spill (v.)
staff
stain
success
sweet (= childlike)
trouble (get into ...)
visual
Whoops!

Unit 8

Verbs connected with food and cooking

bake
boil
burn
chop
fry
grate
grill
mash
scramble
slice

attack (n.)
balanced
beat (a record)
bin
breath (hold
  one's ...)
catch fire
crushed
cure
curry
desperate
diet (n.)
dirt
drop off
earth (What on ...?)
either (modifier)
eventually
fertilizers
flame
gas
gently
get the sack (= lose
  one's job)
give a hand
  (= help)
grill (n. and v.)
harmful
hiccups
iron (n.)
ironing
multi-vitamin
necessary
Ouch!
overcook
paper bag
pat (v.)
pesticides
pill
record holder
sausage
shock (n. and v.)
slow down
sneeze
sniff
supplement
tablet
takeaway
tap (n.)
tea towel
tender
turn off

Unit 9

Nouns and adjectives of emotion

happiness – happy
jealousy – jealous
loneliness – lonely
misery – miserable
nastiness – nasty
nervousness –
  nervous
shyness – shy

bother (Don't ...)
bullying
call someone
  names
commit (a crime)
creep (n.)
crime
dare
defend
driving test
fun (make ... of)
likely
miss (= be absent)
motorbike
pay back (money)
pick on someone
posh
reason (for no ...)
rental shop
trip someone up
upset (easily ...)
victim
weak point

Unit 10

air fare
authorities
Belgian
Black Sea
Channel Tunnel
China
claim (v.) (= state)
Colombia
communicate
consul
cruise (n.)
deaf and dumb
deceive
hitchhike
homesick
Hong Kong
household name
Laos
luxury (adj.)
Malaysia
official (n.)
orphan
Panama
passport
punish
Russia
safely

secretly
settle down
sign language
Singapore
social services
stowaway (n.)
stow away (v.)
survive
Thailand
Venezuela
Vietnam
whether

Unit 11

Verb get

a newspaper/
  a phone call/
  good marks
angry/better
changed/dressed/
  engaged
to bed/to Paris /
  to school/to work

Parts of the body

affection
asleep
average (on ...)
bowl (v.)
break (have a ...)
chemicals
Clear off!
corner shop
cuddle (v.)
deal (It's a ...)
definitely
energy
evidence
expose
generation
growth
hormone
injury
interfere
investigate
late-developer
maximum
myth
non-smoking
potential
pregnant
previous
produce (= make
  naturally)
release
smoke (v.)
store (v.)
stressed
strike (in bowling)
switch off
tall (a ... story)
theme

Unit 12

Adjectives to describe behaviour

rude
sensible
stupid
(im)polite
(un)critical
(un)friendly
(un)helpful
(un)kind

battery (n. and adj.)
break down
  (of a car)
cage
calf
champagne
claw
commercial (TV ...)
concrete
corn
crate
crops
damage (v.)
deliver
demand (n.)
drop out
exist
export (v.)
factory
farmyard
fault
feather
fibre
flap (v.)
force (v.)
free-range
graze
hen
hygienic
intensive
iron (= mineral)
lay (eggs)
liquid
locally
lock up
low (in iron)
marmalade
method
olive
organic
peck (v.)
predator
produce
production line
properly
protest (v.)
reality
recipient
refund
repair
scratch (v.)
sharp
shrink
sloping

space
stack
straw
stretch (v.)
surely
treat (v.)
turn round
veal
wheat
wine
wing
wire

Unit 13

Personality adjectives

aggressive
bossy
emotional
lighthearted
loud
outgoing
practical
quick-tempered
quiet
reliable
romantic
sensitive
serious
shy
sociable

appearance
behaviour
charity
cheer someone up
depressed
education
exotic
fed up with
flirt (v.)
forgive
homeless (n.)
Indonesia
item
Japan
later on
mile (run a ...)
partner
president
prime minister
private
property
recognise someone
regret
relationship
row (have a ... with)
run away with
sake
  (for goodness' ...)
social
suspicious
teach someone a
  lesson
time capsule
waste (v.)

Unit 14

Types of music

box office
change
  (one's mind)
chat (have a ...)
claim (v.)
  (a possession)
Disgusting!
end (in the ...)
essay
hardly
let someone do
  something
pick up
  (= give a lift to)
pitch (a tent)
ring (v.) (= phone)
sleeping bag
stall

Unit 15

acrobat
audience
backstage
clown
contort
contortionist
current
else (anything ...)
enthral
exclude
far and wide
  (from ...)
fire-eater
hand-balancing act
intense
make someone do
  something
mention
pole
stilt-walker
street-performer
swing (v.)
tight-wire artist
trapeze
trick (n.)
troupe
unique
wardrobe assistant

Unit 16

Word-building from different parts of speech

act – acting – actor
build – building – builder
cook – cooking – cooker
drive – driving – driver
heat – heating – heater
paint – painting – painter
sing – singing – singer
smuggle – smuggling – smuggler

ashore
Australia
avoid
barrel
better (I'd ...)
bootlegger
brandy
card (playing ...)
card (student ...)
cart
catch (= capture)
catch (n.) (fish)
central heating
command (n.)
common
contraband
copper
copy (of a newspaper)
Cornish
cover (v.)
customs officers
disguise (v.)
duty
entry
fishermen
gallop
goods
grease
hide (v. tr. and intr.)
lace
like (look ...)
living (make a ...)
magic
mine (n.)
obey
over-fishing
overseas
pair
particularly
pilchards
pleasure boat
pollution
rate

reasons (for health ...)
Roman Empire
rocky
roof
slam
slippery
stockings
sunflower
tin
top hat
trade (v.)
transport (v.)
trick (v.)
warm (v.)

Unit 17

Noun formation with endings
-ment, -ion, -er, -ance

achievement
entertainment
equipment
government

communication
demonstration
education
invention
relation

receiver
transmitter
winner

distance
importance
performance

adopt
aerial
astonish
attic
believe (their ears)
birth
close down
curve (n.)
distress (in ...)
English Channel
fantastic
fire (a gun)
get through (on the phone)
join (= be part of group)
kite
military
monopoly
multi-millionaire
navy
Newfoundland
open-air theatre
recognise (= be aware of)
radar
respect (mark of ...)

satellite
shore (ship to ...)
signal (n.)
telegraph
transmit
twice (think ...)
wave (radio ...)
wireless

Unit 18

Phrases of approximate time
about (two days)
a couple of (days)
a few (days)
several (days)
(not) for some time
(not) for ages

Phrases of approximate quantity
about (three people)
a couple of (people)
a few (people)
several (people)
lots of (people)
loads of (people)
hundreds/ thousands of (people)

army
background (in the ...)
behind (stay ...)
board up
crash (n.)
divide
extract
flock of birds
gull
heavy (rain)
host
natural
now and again
pale
seagull
setting
shake
shoot
short story
switch on
van
vet

Unit 19

Neutral and strong adjectives
afraid – terrified
bad – terrible
big – enormous
good – brilliant

hungry – starving
small – tiny
tired – exhausted

attitude
contest
deal (business ...)
driving test
fantasy
finals
flight
fortune
give up
hang gliding
irritate
jet (n.)
knock off
make someone laugh
medal
obviously
perfectionist
prize money
rapper
regards
rival
title
turning point
wait around
wish (n.)

Unit 20

ability
back (get ... in the water)
before our eyes
break (a silence)
breakthrough
celebrity
conventional
correspondent
deprived of
despair (in ...)
desperation (in ...)
dolphin
eventually
expect someone to do something
get someone to do something
grab
lack of confidence
lifelong
link
magical
marvellous
mend
motivate
overcome
oxygen
physical
raise money
seize
session
silence
simply

speech therapy
stammer
starved of
strength (from ... to ...)
technique
therapist
though (even ...)
treatment
unexpected

Irregular verbs

Infinitive	Past simple	Past participle
be	was	been
beat	beat	beaten
become	became	become
begin	began	begun
bite	bit	bitten
blow	blew	blown
break	broke	broken
bring	brought	brought
build	built	built
burn	burnt/burned	burnt/burned
buy	bought	bought
catch	caught	caught
choose	chose	chosen
come	came	come
cost	cost	cost
cut	cut	cut
do	did	done
draw	drew	drawn
dream	dreamt/dreamed	dreamt/dreamed
drink	drank	drunk
drive	drove	driven
eat	ate	eaten
fall	fell	fallen
feed	fed	fed
feel	felt	felt
fight	fought	fought
find	found	found
fly	flew	flown
forget	forgot	forgotten
freeze	froze	frozen
get	got	got
give	gave	given
go	went	gone
grow	grew	grown
have	had	had
hear	heard	heard
hide	hid	hidden
hit	hit	hit
hold	held	held
hurt	hurt	hurt
keep	kept	kept
know	knew	known
lay	laid	laid
lead	led	led
leap	leapt	leapt
learn	learnt/learned	learnt/learned
leave	left	left
lend	lent	lent
let	let	let
lie	lay	lain
lose	lost	lost
make	made	made
mean	meant	meant
meet	met	met
pay	paid	paid
put	put	put
read	read	read
ride	rode	ridden
ring	rang	rung
rise	rose	risen
run	ran	run
say	said	said

Infinitive	Past simple	Past participle
see	saw	seen
sell	sold	sold
send	sent	sent
set	set	set
shake	shook	shaken
shine	shone	shone
shoot	shot	shot
show	showed	shown/showed
shrink	shrank/shrunk	shrunk
shut	shut	shut
sing	sang	sung
sink	sank	sunk
sit	sat	sat
sleep	slept	slept
smell	smelt	smelt
speak	spoke	spoken
spend	spent	spent
spill	spilt	spilt
split (up)	split (up)	split (up)
spread	spread	spread
stand	stood	stood
steal	stole	stolen
strike	struck	struck
sweep	swept	swept
swim	swam	swum
swing	swung	swung
take	took	taken
teach	taught	taught
tear	tore	torn
tell	told	told
think	thought	thought
throw	threw	thrown
understand	understood	understood
wake (up)	woke (up)	woken (up)
wear	wore	worn
weep	wept	wept
win	won	won
write	wrote	written

Acknowledgements

We are grateful to the following for permission to reproduce copyright material:
authors' agents (Curtis Brown Ltd) on behalf of the Chichester Partnership for a printed/recorded extract from the short story 'The Birds' by Daphne Du Maurier, simplified by Lewis Jones in THE DREAM AND OTHER STORIES, published by Addison Wesley Longman Ltd 1997. Copyright Daphne Du Maurier 1952; Guardian News Services Ltd for an adapted extract from the article 'Miami dolphins help mute British boy to speak' by Sara Bosely in THE GUARDIAN 27.3.98. Polygram/Music Sales Ltd for the lyrics to 'I will survive' by Frederick Perren & Dino Fekaris. ©1978 Polygram Music Publishing Ltd; Rondor Music for the lyrics to 'California Girls' by Wilson & Love. ©1965 by Irving Music Inc; Solo Syndication for adapted extracts from the articles 'Scuba hero rescues drowning motorist' by Daily Mail Reporter in THE DAILY MAIL 9.8.97, 'Boy who was taught to talk by a dolphin' by Daily Mail Reporter in THE DAILY MAIL 27.3.98, 'The Greatest Show under the Soleil' by Nick Curtis in THE EVENING STANDARD 15.1.97, 'The Super Stowaway' by Nick Buckley & Andrew Chapman in THE MAIL ON SUNDAY 22.12.96; Sony/ATV Music for the lyrics to 'When I'm sixty-four' by John Lennon and Paul McCartney © 1967 Northern Songs. All rights controlled by MCA Music Ltd under licence from Northern Songs; News International Newspapers Ltd for adapted extracts from the articles 'Climbing is our Life' by Annabelle Jones & Claire Hippert in THE TIMES 1015 section 20.9.97. ©Annabelle Jones/Clare Hippert/The Times, London 1997 & 'Swing Out Sister' by Louise Johncox from THE TIMES 1015 section 20.12.97. ©Louise Johncox/The Times, London 1997.

We are grateful to the following for permission to use copyright photographs:

ACE Photo Agency for pages 21 (bottom left), 118 (top left, top right, middle); ©AWL/by Trevor Clifford for pages 14 (left), 48 (bottom left); The Anthony Blake Photo Library for page 90 (middle left, bottom left, bottom right); ©BMW (GB) Ltd for page 30 (lower middle right); The British Museum for page 45 (top middle); Britstock-IFA for pages 11 (top right), 30 (top middle left); Camera Press for page 100 (main); Capital Pictures for page 32 (bottom left); Cirque du Soleil Alegria/Al Sieb/Dominique Lemieux for pages 88 (left), 89; Collections for pages 20 (bottom left), 52; Colorific for page 21 (upper bottom); Alan Copson for page 21 (lower middle); Dewynters plc for page 45 (top right, bottom left); Daphne Du Maurier, Rebecca, Arrow Books for page 21 (lower top); Greg Evans International for pages 11 (bottom right), 21 (bottom right), 24 (right inset), 101 (bottom right); Mary Evans Picture Library for pages 92 (middle left), 93 (top), 95 (middle & bottom); Famous/Duval for page 46 (bottom right); FLPA for pages 30 (top middle right), 32 (bottom right); Fortean Picture Library for page 62 (top right); Ronald Grant Archive for pages 46 (middle left, middle right, bottom left), 62 (bottom); Robert Harding Picture Library for pages 21 (upper middle), 34 (top main, top right , middle left, middle right, bottom left); Crown copyright: Historic Royal Palaces for page 45 (top left); Hulton Getty Picture Collection for page 100 (inset); Annabelle Jones for page 18; Kobal Collection for page 58 (top, upper middle),/Fox 1996 for page 112 (bottom); London Features International for page 46 (lower top); Madame Tussaud's for page 45 (middle); McCabes for page 96 (left); Jeff Morris for pages 60 (top), 61 (bottom); by kind permission of Murray King Studio St Ives Cornwall for page 95 (top); National Museums & Galleries on Merseyside for pages 92 (top left & bottom left), 93 (bottom); Natural History Museum for page 45 (bottom right); Network for pages 24 (main), 84 (bottom left inset); People in Pictures for pages 76 (bottom right), 112 (main); Pictor International for pages 10, 24 (top left inset), 30 (bottom left), 32 (middle left), 54 (left), 76 (top left), 77 (bottom); Popperfoto for page 105; Redferns for page 84 (middle); Rex Features for pages 12, 30 (top middle, lower top left, lower top right, middle left, bottom middle left), 58 (lower middle, bottom), 62 (top left, middle left), 76 (bottom middle), 84-85 (bottom), 88 (bottom right), 90 (top left, top middle, top right), 102 (top right); RSPCA Photo Library for page 73; Science Museum/Science & Society Picture Library for page 101 (bottom left); Solent News & Photo Agency for page 36; South West News Service for pages 116, 117; The Stock Market Photo Agency Inc for pages 6-7, 20-21 (top), 26-27; Tony Stone Images for pages 11 (top left), 21 (top), 30 (top left, bottom right), 32-33, 50 (middle), 76 (bottom left, middle right, middle), 84 (top), 102, 118 (bottom middle left); Superstock for page 46 (top); Sygma for page 112 (middle); Tate Gallery for page 96 (right); Telegraph Colour Library for pages 11 (middle, bottom left), 20 (middle left, bottom middle), 30 (bottom middle), 76 (top right), 79, 118 (bottom left, bottom middle right, bottom right); Topham Picturepoint for pages 30 (top right, bottom middle right), 95 (lower top).

We are unable to trace the copyright holder of the photograph on page 54 (right) and would be grateful for any information to enable us to do so.

All photographs not listed above are ©AWL/by Peter Lake.

Cover photographs: ©AWL/Peter Lake (main camera); The Ronald Grant Archive (bottom left); Robert Harding Picture Library/Roy Rainford (middle left); Image Bank (bottom right); Annabelle Jones (middle right); Tony Stone Images/Roberts Everts (upper top right); Telegraph Colour Library/Planet Earth/D. Robert Franz (lower top left).

Our special thanks to the following for their help during location photography: Buzz Cooperative Ltd; Cornish Delights, Newquay; Country Goodness, Newquay; Fistral Chef, Newquay; Fistral Surf Company Ltd, Newquay; Headlands Hotel, Port Isaac; Little Big Chippy, Newquay; Lloyds Lane Bowling Alley, Enfield; Market House Hotel, Sawbridgeworth; Minack Theatre, Porthcurno; Naturally Wood Furniture; North Weald Police Station.